HISTORIC
EGYPT

ESCUDO DE ORO

HISTORIC EGYPT

Text: Mohamed Hassan
English translation: Alan Moore
Photographs: Enrique Soldevilla, Kerolos Barsoum and Lehnert & Landrock

Design, lay-out and printing completely created
by the technical department of
EDITORIAL FISA ESCUDO DE ORO, S.A.

Classical historians, Roman emperors, Arab travellers, adventurers, millions of tourists, all these have heard a voice from afar, calling them to these lands to witness the greatness of an ancient and mysterious civilisation. Just imagine, just think what life must have been like in the times of the Pharaohs: the glittering pyramids and the richly decorated temples; or in Islamic times, the air full of eastern aromas and the voices of the muezzins resounding all around. Only one country can offer all this: **Egypt**.

INTRODUCTION

Night-time view of Cairo city centre.

Night-time view of the Pyramid of Cheops.

Geographic situation, climate and population

The Arab Republic of Egypt, the official name of the country, or MISR, as it is known in Arabic, lies in northeast Africa, occupying an area of nearly one million square kilometres. The country, which has a maximum distance of 1,055 km from north to south and 1,250 km from east to west, is divided by the world's longest river, the Nile. In Egypt, the Nile runs for 1,508 km, creating a green strip on either side, though this represents just 4% of the country's total surface area. Stretching to the east of the river is the Arabian Desert, whilst to the west is the Libyan Desert, which forms part of the Sahara. The country's coastline is bathed by the waters of the Mediterranean to the north and by the Red Sea to the east. The Sinai Peninsula is a part of Egypt that lies in Asia, separated from the African continent by the Suez Canal. Egypt lies between 31° 30' latitude north at the Nile Delta and Parallel 22 on the frontier with Sudan.

The climate in country varies its geography. In the south, summers are almost tropical, with temperatures of over 40° C during the day, though the nights are a little cooler. In the north the temperature is about 32° C. On the other hand, the southern winter is characterised by pleasant temperatures of around 20° C during the day, but colder nights. In the north, as in all Mediterranean countries, temperatures fall in winter.

The population of Egypt is around 75 million, 90% are Muslims and the remaining 10% Christians. Men make up 50.5% of the population (with average life expectancy of 65.4 years), whilst women account for 49.5% (with average life expectancy of 69.5 years). As for natural growth, families have an average of 2.5 children. The ethnic characteristics of the population are similar to their neighbours in southern Mediterranean countries, though with certain variants due to successive invasions, particularly by Arab peoples (Semites).

Temple of Ramses II and Lake Nasser. Abu Simbel.

Mist cloaks the River Nile and the temple in a special atmosphere. Luxor.

Feluccas at dusk. Aswan.

 Camels carrying sugar cane. Tuna El-Gebel.

Palm trees at the Oasis of Bahariya.

Wheat is one of Egypt's main crops.

The Nile: flora and fauna

According to Herodotus, the classical historian of the 5th century BC, Egypt is a gift of the Nile. The river has watered Egypt's lands since immemorial time, replenished by rain falling in the Ethiopian mountains and on Lake Victoria, where it has its source. Every August, minerals were carried down with the river mud, fertilising the land all around during the flood season. Nowadays, the Nile's flooding is controlled by the Aswan Dam, but Egypt continues to be principally an agricultural country.

Egypt's flora also varies greatly due to climate. Though there are few trees, this is a country rich in fruits and vegetables, where such tropical fruits as mango and guava flourish as well as the most important palm tree, the date palm. Egypt boasts over seven million date palms, producing more than 15 types of date. Other common trees in Egypt include the acacia and the sycamore, as well as other typical Mediterranean species such as oranges and banana trees. The main crops are sugar cane, wheat, maize, tomatoes, rice, oranges and cotton.

Egyptian fauna is also highly varied. Amongst domestic animals, sheep are the most common, followed by goats, Egyptian buffaloes, cows, donkeys and camels. In the Egyptian desert, though in ever decreasing numbers, it is still possible to see other mammals, such as ibex, and reptiles, including the Egyptian cobra. There are many bird species here too, including falcons, herons, crows and swallows.

Cultivated fields around Luxor.

Buffalo.

Ibex.

Cobra.

Falcon.

HISTORICAL SUMMARY

The first settlements go back to the Neolithic Age. By around 5500 BC, the Nile was fairly stable, and humans came to dwell near its waters, forming the first civilisations towards the end of the Fifth Millennium, in around 4800 BC, at first around what is now el Fayum and later in the Nile Delta and in the south of the country. Little by little, two kingdoms came into being. The first, in the north, or Lower Egypt, had Buto as its capital, and goddess Wadjit, who took the form of a cobra was its chief deity, whilst the monarchs wore a red crown. The other kingdom, Upper Egypt, was in the south. Its capital was Nekhen and its deity was the goddess Nekhbet, who took the form of a vulture. The kings of Upper Egypt wore a conical white crown.

■ Statue of Zhoser. Egyptian Museum of Cairo.

The Time of the Pharaohs

It was the Egyptian priest Maneton who classified the Pharaohs into 30 dynasties when Ptolemy II com-

missioned him to write the history of Egypt in 280 BC. Since then, historians across the ages have all followed Maneton's chronology.

In around 3000 BC, Narmer became ruler of both Upper and Lower Egypt, unifying the two kingdoms for the first time. For this reason, Narmer is also known as Menes, which means "founder". Narmer also ordered the construction of Egypt's first capital, Memphis, situated just before the Nile divides into two branches to form the Delta. Thus began what is known as the Archaic Period, which ended in 2670 BC. That same year marks the beginning of the Old Kingdom or Pyramid Period. Its first ruler was the celebrated Pharaoh Djoser (Zoser), head of the 3rd Dynasty and builder of the Saqqara Step Pyramid. Later, Egypt was governed by the Pharaohs of the 4th Dynasty: Sneferu, Cheops,

■ Pyramids of Cheops, Chephren and Mycerinus.

Chephren and Mycerinus, whose magnificent pyramids are found in Giza and Dahshur. However, a peaceful transition to the rule of the Sun Kings occurred during the 5th Dynasty, and these preferred to build their pyramids and mortuary temples in the Abu Sir area. At the end of the 6th Dynasty, Egypt suffered a great drought, which caused famine in the land, a situation that led to civil war, sowing the seeds of complete chaos in the country's central government in 2198 BC. These times of crisis are known as the First Intermediary Period and lasted until 2008 BC. The country was finally pacified and unified once more under Mentuhotep II (Nebhepetra), of the 11th

■ Statue of Mentuhotep II. Egyptian Museum of Cairo.

Dynasty, and boats once more began to sail up and down the Nile. A period of stability known as the Middle Kingdom began under this Pharaoh.

At first, the capital was Thebes, but the Pharaohs of the 12th Dynasty built another near Memphis, naming it Itj-Tawy, on the site of what is now E-Lisht. During the period of transition between the two capitals, the Pharaohs continued as before to be buried in pyramids, but these began to be built from mud bricks and covered with stones. Over time, the stones were lost, and the pyramid became a pile of clay. At the same time, the Pharaohs were expanding to the south in search of gold in Nubia, where several temples were built, and held in enormous esteem by later Pharaohs.

The Middle Kingdom period is one of the richest for Egyptian art. An excellent example of this are the reliefs of Senwosret I, the statues of Amenemhet I and Amenemhet III and, above all, the scenes that decorate the tombs at Beni Hassan.

The Pharaohs of this period attached great importance to agricultural development, particularly in the el Fayum area, as well as such projects as the plan to join the Nile and the Red Sea via the Sesostris Canal (Senwosret III). The ancient Egyptians wrote novels like *The Shipwrecked Sailor* and *Sinuhy* on papyrus, and in modern times these provided inspiration for Mika Waltari's novel *Sinuhe The Egyptian*, amongst others. The many jewels belonging to princesses, exhib-

Pyramid of El Lisht. ■

■ Bust of Queen Hatshepsut. Egyptian Museum of Cairo.

ty; his son Akhenaten (Amenophis IV), the world's first monotheist ruler, well known for his religious revolution; Akhenaten's wife, Nefertiti, and, of course, Tutankhamun, whose treasures fill and enrich the Egyptian Museum in Cairo.

During the 19th Dynasty, the Pharaohs Seti I and Ramses II continued the military campaigns launched by their predecessors. In terms of art, Seti left us the most beautiful reliefs from the times of the Pharaohs in his temples and tomb, whilst Ramses built such huge architectural wonders as the Temple of Abu Simbel. Ramses III is also considered one of the most important Pharaohs during this period due to his military campaigns and architectural enterprises.

Egypt began to fall into decline in the late-11th century BC, despite the efforts of Taharqa, during the

Statue of Akhenaton. Egyptian Museum of Cairo. ■

ited in the Egyptian Museum in Cairo and in the Metropolitan Museum, provide clear evidence of Egypt's development in those times.

The Second Intermediary Period, which began in around 1630 BC, was marked by the invasion of the Hyksos, coming from eastern Asia. The country was divided at that time between many different dynasties. The Hyksos surprised the Egyptians with their bronze weapons which much harder than those used by the Egyptians, as well as a new weapon: chariots, each drawn by two horses. The Hyksos, who worshipped the god Set, ruled Egypt for about 108 years, establishing their capital in the eastern area of the Delta.

It was the rulers of Egypt's fourth province, Thebes, who fought against the Hyksos until they finally overcame the invader in the so-called wars of liberation. First Seqenenre, Pharaoh of the 17th Dynasty, then his son, Kamose, and finally his other son, Ahmose, waged war on the Hyksos, freeing the country and founding the New Kingdom in 1539 BC.

The New Kingdom period is now considered Egypt's golden age, particularly due to the territories all around that were conquered to form a huge empire stretching from the Euphrates in the northeast to the fourth cataract of the Nile in the south.

Several Pharaohs from the 18th Dynasty engraved their names both on history and on the reliefs found in the ruins of their capital, Thebes or Luxor. Particularly important were Hatshepsut, one of the great female rulers in the history of Egypt; Thutmose III, considered the Napoleon of Ancient Egypt; Amenophis III, the Pharaoh of peace and prosperi-

Statue of Ramses II, reused by Panejem (21st Dynasty). Temple of Karnak, Luxor.

Relief of Cleopatra VII and her son Caesarion. Temple of Denderah.

ing Mark Antony's defeat at the hands of Octavian and the death of Caesarion, the son of Julius Caesar and Cleopatra VII, Egypt became one of the Roman Empire's richest provinces in terms of agriculture, becoming known as "Rome's granary".

Christian Egypt

Saint Mark, who arrived in Alexandria in around 56 AD, slowly and secretly set about inviting the Egyptians to convert to Christianity. Many did so, and were persecuted by the Romans, particularly during the rule

Church and mosque. Cairo.

25th Dynasty, and Psammetichus and Nekau, of the 26th, to restore the country's former splendour, and Egypt was finally occupied by the Persians.

The Graeco-Roman period

Alexander the Great conquered Egypt in the year 332 BC. The Egyptians accepted him as, unlike the Persians, he respected their religion and mythology. On Alexander's death in 323 BC, Ptolemy, son of Lagos, came to the country, and was crowned king in 304 BC. Thus began the Greek Dynasty, with 15 kings, all taking the name of Ptolemy, and a queen, Cleopatra VII. From the country's new capital, Alexandria, the most important city in the Mediterranean at the time, the Ptolemies ruled a country that had now become very rich. This wealth and prosperity is reflected in the temples they built at Edfu and Philae, and those they began to build but were finally completed during Roman times at Kom Ombo, Esna and Dendera. The lighthouse, one of the Seven Wonders of the World, now lost, was built in Alexandria, as well as its famous Library, the most important of a kind in the ancient world, along with the university.

In 30 BC, after the suicide of Cleopatra VII follow-

Ruins of El Fustat.

of Diocletian, who ordered thousands to be martyred in the year 284, considered the first year in the Coptic Calendar in Egypt. Later, when Christianity became the dominant religion under the Byzantine Empire, some ancient temples were converted into churches and monasteries.

The Islamic period

In 640 AD, Amr Ibn El-Ass, leader of the Arab army, conquered Egypt and, after many battles, turned the country into a Muslim state, governed from the Caliphate capital in Arabia. Amr Ibn-El-Ass built El-Fustat, the first Arabic capital of Egypt very close to the place where the Delta and the Valley of the Nile meet, and ordered the construction of Africa's first mosque, which bears his name. Later, during the Umayyad period (658-750), Egypt was ruled from Damascus, whilst under the Abbasids (750-877) the country was governed form Baghdad. In 877, Ibn Tulun established the first independent State of Egypt, ordering the construction of a new capital known as Al-Qatai, a little to the north of El-Fustat, where he built his monumental mosque.

Friday prayers. Cairo. ■

In 969, the Fatimids took over Egypt, building their royal residence next to El- Fustat and Al-Qatai and naming it el Kahira, which means "the victorious". From which the name Cairo derives. Egypt now entered its most flourishing period in terms of Islamic art and architecture.

In 1171, Saladin founded the Ayyubid Dynasty in Egypt. This general of Kurdish origin led the wars against the Crusades, restoring Jerusalem to the Muslims in 1187. Saladin also joined the Islamic capitals of El-Fustat, Al-Qatai and El-Kahira into a single city under the name of Cairo, ordering the construction of a citadel to protect it. In order to control their vast empire, which stretched as far as Syria, the last Ayyubid kings began to buy Turkish-Circassian slaves known as Mamelukes ("slave" in Arabic), but in the year 1250 these finally took power in the country. The Mamelukes made Egypt the most important centre in the world for Islamic art and architecture, leaving considerable evidence of this in the mosques and other buildings they built in Cairo. The first

Minaret in the El-Fath mosque. Cairo. ■

Mameluke sultans enjoyed enormous power, defeating the Mongol armies of none other than Genghis Khan, as well as emerging victorious from the crusades that followed. Finally, however, they were unable to resist the advancing Ottomans, who were beginning to amass a huge empire. Selim I conquered Egypt in 1517, and the country became an annex of the Ottoman Empire, ruled from Istanbul, and the finest Egyptian artists and architects were sent there to make the Ottoman capital as beautiful as Cairo. The period of Ottoman rule ended in 1798 when Napoleon Bonaparte invaded Egypt in order to cut off England's route to its colonies in India. This military campaign served to highlight Egypt's strategic importance in world communications.

The modern and contemporary period

The French remained in Egypt only three years, but wrote a book, the *Description de l'Egipte*, containing past and present studies of the country and awakening interest in a civilisation that had become practically forgotten, whilst the French occupation aroused the Egyptian people's interest in western technology. For this reason when, in 1805, after the departure of the French, a Turkish Albanian, Mohammed

■ The Citadel of Saladin. Cairo.

Ali, came to power, first as governor and later as king in a monarchy he himself established, plans to modernise the country began to be laid. Many irrigation projects were launched, including the construction of the Delta dam, and new crops, principally cotton, were introduced. Factories were installed and a new education system launched, whilst a well-trained and equipped army was prepared. Mohammed Ali's successors continued along these same lines, particularly King Ismael, who had studied in Paris and aspired to make Egypt a modern country on a par with France. King Ismael oversaw many changes, especially in the city of Cairo, and his reign saw the opening of the Suez Canal (1869). Nonetheless, in order to finance this enormous project Egypt fell into debt with Great Britain, which did not pass up the opportunity to interfere in the country's internal affairs, finally occupying Egypt militarily in 1882.

Despite the improvements the British introduced in Egypt æin their own interests, it must be saidæ such as building a better irrigation system from the old Aswan Dam and the dams at Esna and Naga Hamadi in order to grow cotton, or the construction of the first railway line between Alexandria and Aswan for troop transport, the British occupation did nothing more than fuel the population's desire for independence. This was finally granted in 1922, though under British

control, and the country ruled over by King Fuad and his son and successor Farouk was unstable both economically and politically. More and more, the people demanded a free Egypt, governed by its own citizens. This situation culminated in the Revolution of 23 July 1952, when King Farouk was removed from the throne and the Republic declared (18 June 1953). The first president was Mohammed Naguib, who was succeeded in 1954 by Lieutenant Colonel Gamal Abdul Nasser. Nasser built the Aswan Dam, nationalised the Suez Canal and helped many African and Arabic countries to achieve independence. In 1967, however, Egypt's defeat at the hands of Israel in the Six Days War resulted in the loss of the Sinai Peninsula and the blockade of the Suez Canal.

When Nasser died in 1970, vice-president Anwar El-Sadat was elected as president by plebiscite. Sadat came to government at a time when morale in the country was low, but Egypt's victory in the short-fought Yum Kippur war in October 1973 persuaded Israel to sign a peace agreement. In this way, El-Sadat won the world's respect, as he had saved bloodshed on both sides as well as regaining Sinai. However, some were opposed to this peace, particularly the fundamentalists, and some of these, having infiltrated the army, assassinated El-Sadat on the day of victory celebrations in 1981. Since then, Egypt has been

The Hotel Marriott, a palace built by Ismael. Cairo. ■

Tomb of Anwar El Sadat and monument to the unknown soldier. Cairo. ■

CHRONOLOGY OF ANCIENT EGYPT

This chronology of Ancient Egypt, the one most widely accepted by historians, includes a list of the most important monarchs. From the 12th Dynasty on, between brackets, is the title with which they were crowned.

Dynasty 0
Irihor (?)
"Scorpion"   circa 3050 BC
Narmer

ARCHAIC PERIOD

Dynasty 1 – c. 3000-2800
Aha (Athothis)
Djer (Kenkenes)
Wadj (Uenephes)
Den (Usaphais)
Adjib (Miebis)
Semerkhet (Semempses)
Qaa (Ubienthes)

Dynasty 2 – c. 2800-2670
Hetepsekhmwy
Reneb
Ninetjer
Peribsen
Khasekhem

OLD KINGDOM

Dynasty 3 – c. 2670-2600
Nebka
Djoser   2654-2635
Sekhemkhet
Huni   2625-2600

Dynasty 4 – c. 2600-2487
Snofru   2600-2571
Khufu (Cheops)   2571-2548
Radjedef   2548-2540
Khephren (Khafre)   2540-2514
Menkaure (Mycerinos)   2510-2491
Shepseskaf   2491-2487

Dynasty 5 – c. 2487-2348
Userkaf   2487-2480
Sahure   2480-2468
Neferirkare   2468-2449
Neuserre   2443-2419
Menkauhor   2419-2411
Djedkare (Izezi)   2411-2378
Wenis   2378-2348

Dynasty 6 – c. 2348-2198
Teti   2348-2320
Userkare
Pepy I (Meryre)   2316-2284
Merenre I   2284-2270
Pepy II (Neferkare)   2270-2205
Merenre II. Antyemzaf
Nitocris (?)

FIRST INTERMEDIATE PERIOD

Dynasties 7 and 8 – c. 2198-2160
Several ephemeral rulers

Dynasties 9 and 10 – c. 2160-1980
Kheti III
Merykare

Dynasty 11 – c. 2081-1938
Inyotef I (Sehertawy)   2081-2065
Inyotef II (Wahankh)   2065-2016
Inyotef III (Nakhtnebtepnufer)   2016-2008
Mentuhotpe I (Nebhhepetre)   2008-1957
Mentuhotpe II (Sankhkare)   1957-1945
Mentuhotpe III (Nebtawyre)   1945-1938

MIDDLE KINGDOM

Dynasty 12 – c. 1938-1759
Amenemhet I (Sehetepibre)   1938-1909
Senwosret I (Kheperkare)   1909-1875
Amenemhet II (Nubkaure)   1877-1843
Senwosret II (Khakheperre)   1845-1837
Senwosret III (Khakaure)   1837-1818
Amenemhet III (Nimaatre)   1818-1773
Amenemhet IV (Maakherure)   1773-1763
Nefrusobk (Nefru Sobek Shedty)   1763-1759

SECOND INTERMEDIATE PERIOD

Dynasty 13 – c. 1759-1630
(1) Wegaf (Khutawyre)   1759-1757
(12) Sebekhotpe I (Khaankhre)
(14) Awibre
(16) Sebekhotpe II (Sekhemre-khutawy)
(17) Khendjer (Userkare)
(21) Sebekhotpe III (Sekhemre-swadjtawy)
(22) Neferhotep (Khasekhemre)   1705-1694
(24) Sebekhotpe IV (Khaneferre)   1694-1685
(27) Aya (Merneferre)

Dynasty 14 – c. 1700-1630
Nehesy and other minor kings in the delta

Dynasties 15 and 16 (Hyksos) – c. 1630-1522
Salitis (Sekhaenre?)
Bnon
Apachnan / Khiyan (Swosererne)
Iannas / Yinassi
Arkhles / Sikruhaddu
Apophis (Awoserre)   1573-1533
Khamudi   1533-1522

Dynasty 17 (Theban) – c. 1640-1539
Inyotef (Nubkheperre)   c. 1630
Tao I (Senakhtenre)   c. 1570
Tao II (?) (Seqenenre)   c. 1560/50
Kamose (Wadjkheperre)   1543-1539

NEW KINGDOM

Dynasty 18 – c. 1539-1292
Ahmose (Nebpehtire)	1539-1514
Amenophis I (Djeserkare)	1514-1493
Tuthmosis I (Akheperkare)	1493-1482
Tuthmosis II (Akheperenre)	1482-1479
Hatshepsut (Maatkare)	1479-1458
Tuthmosis III (Menkheperre)	1479-1426
Amenophis II (Akheprure)	1426-1400
Tuthmosis IV (Menkheprure)	1400-1390
Amenophis III (Nebmaatre)	1390-1353
Amenophis IV / Akhenaten (Neferkheprure)	1353-1336
Smenkhkhare (Ankhkheprure)	1336-1333
Tutankhamun (Nebkheprure)	1333-1323
Aya (Kheperkheprure)	1323-1319
Haremhab (Djeserkheprure)	1319-1292

Dynasty 19 (early Ramesside Period) – c. 1292-1188
Ramses I (Menpehtire)	1292-1290
Sethos I (Menmaatre)	1290-1279
Ramses II (Usermaatre setepenre)	1279-1213
Merneptah (Baenre meritamun)	1213-1203
Sethos II (Userkheprure setepenre)	1203-1196
Amenmesse (Menmire)	
Siptah (Akhenre setepenre)	1196-1190
Twosre (Sitre meritamun)	1190-1188

Dynasty 20 (late Ramesside Period) – c. 1188-1075
Sekhnakhte (Userkhaure meryamun)	1188-1186
Ramses III (Usermaatre meryamun)	1186-1155
Ramses IV (Heqamaatre setepenamun)	1155-1148
Ramses V (Usermaatre sekheperenre)	1148-1143
Ramses VI (Nebmaatre meryamun)	1143-1135
Ramses VII (Usermaatre setepenre meryamun)	1135-1129
Ramses VIII (Usermaatre akhenamun)	1129-1127
Ramses IX (Neterkare setepenre)	1127-1108
Ramses X (Khepermaatre setepenre)	1108-1104
Ramses XI (Menmaatre setepenptah)	1104-1075

THIRD INTERMEDIATE PERIOD

Dynasty 21 – c. 1075-945
Smendes (Hedjkhperre setepenre)	1075-1044
Amenemnisu (Neferkare)	1044-1040
Psusennes I (Akheperre setepenamun)	1040-990
Amenemope (Usermaatre setepenamun)	993-984
Siamun (Netjerkheperre setepenamun)	978-960
Psusennes II (Titkheperre setepenre)	960-945

Dynasty 22 (Bubastids) – c. 945-715
Shoshenq I (Hedjkhperre setepenre)	945-924
Osorkon I (Sekhemkheperre setepenre)	924-889
Takelot I (Hedjkhperre setepenre)	889-874
Osorkon II (Usermaatre setepenamun)	874-850
Takelot II (Hedjkhperre setepenre)	850-825
Shoshenq III (Usermaatre setepenre)	825-773
Pami (Usermaatre setepenre)	773-767
Shoshenq V (Akheperre setepenre)	767-730

Osorkon IV (Akheperre setepenamun)	730-715?
(addiotionally, many local principalities)	

Dynasty 23 – c. 818-715
Pedubaste (Usermaatre setepenamun)	818-793
Soshenq IV (Usermaatre meryamun)	793-787
Osorkon III (Usermaatre setepenamun)	787-759
Takelot III (Usermaatre setepenamun)	764-757
Rudjamun (Usermaatre setepenamun)	757-754
Iupet II (Usermaatre setepenamun)	754-715?
(addiotionally, many local principalities)	

Dynasty 24 – c. 725-712
Tefnakhte (Shepsesre)	725-718
Bocchoris (Wahkare)	718-712

Dynasty 25 (Ethiopian) – c. 712-664
Kashta (Maatre?)	?-740
Piye / Piankhy (?) (Usermaatre and others)	740-713
Shabaka (Neferkare)	712-698
Shebitku (Djedkaure)	698-690
Taharqa (Khunefertemre)	690-664
Tantamani (Bakare)	664-656

Assyryan Conquest – 671-664

LATE PERIOD

Dynasty 26 (Saite) – 664-525
Necho I (Menkheperre)	672-664
Psammetichus I (Wahibre)	664-610
Necho II (Wehemibre)	610-595
Psammetichus II (Neferibre)	595-589
Apries (Haaibre)	589-570
Amasis (Khnemibre)	570-526
Psammetichus III (Ankhkaenre)	526-525

Dynasty 27 (Persian Period) – 525-404

Dynasty 28 – 404-399
Amyrtaios	404-399

Dynasty 29 – 399-380
Nepherites I (Baenre merynetjeru)	399-393
Psammuthis (Userre setepenptah)	393
Hakoris (Khnemmaatre)	393-380
Nepherites II (Baenre merynetjeru)	380

Dynasty 30 – 380-343
Nektanebo (Nakhtnebef) I (Kheperkare)	380-362
Teos (Irmaatenre)	362-360
Nektanebo (Nakhthorehbit) II (Senedjemibre)	360-343

Second Persian Period – 343-332

Macedonians – 332-305

Ptolemaic Period – 305-30

Roman and Byzantine Periods – 30 BC-642 CE

19

governed by President Hosni Mubarak, who follows the line of peace initiated by Sadat, and his country is enjoying the fruits of this in the form of progress and development in all spheres of life.

Social structure

Throughout ancient times, Egypt was an agricultural society settled around the Nile. The base of the country's social structure was formed by peasant farmers, workers and artists. Above these were the mayors, followed, by provincial governors, civil servants, priests and the vizier. All these obeyed the orders passed down from the apex of the pyramid, his majesty the Pharaoh.

The Pharaoh was not only the king, but also a concept and an intermediary between the gods and the people. The Pharaohs possessed five royal names: the first and the third indicated that they governed Egypt as the representative of the god Horus, victorious over his enemies; the second, that they governed with the protection of the gods of the north and south (in the form of the cobra and the vulture, respectively); the fourth, that they reigned as kings of Upper and Lower Egypt; whilst the fifth identified them as the children of Ra, the sun god. The Pharaoh also had two given names, one given at birth, the other on coronation, and these were written in a special oblong frame or enclosure known as a *cartouche.*

In all his representations, the Pharaoh is seen with a false beard symbolising his experience, and a cobra, symbolising protection, on his forehead. The Pharaohs had different crowns. At first, when Egypt was divid-

■ Partial view of the cartouche of Pharaoh Senusret I. Egyptian Museum of Cairo.

ed into two kingdoms, there were two, a conical white crown for southern Egypt and a red one for the king of the north. After the unification of Upper and Lower Egypt, a double crown was used, featuring the same elements, to symbolise this union. Another type of crown was the typical headcloth, known as *nemes* in hieroglyphics. Yet another appeared later: the blue crown of war.

The Pharaoh's robes were made of the finest linen, white in most cases. They took different forms, though the most habitual dress was a tight skirt from waist to knees. On occasions, the Pharaoh is seen holding different types of sceptres, crooks and flails as part of the royal insignia.

The vizier or prime minister was the second person in importance after Pharaoh. The vizier was responsible for the country's administrative organisation, directing the governors of Egypt's 42 provinces, 22 in the south and 20 in the north.

Next came the princes and governors, who might be given the title of "son of the Pharaoh", whether or not they were his natural children. The princes acted as judges and sometimes as the high priest in their respective provinces, as well as governing and collecting taxes for the coffers of the central administration in the Egyptian capital.

The bearers of the Pharaoh's royal seal, sandal and fan were also very important, and considered fortunate to be so close to the ruler. Only those with the title "sole companion of the Pharaoh" were placed above these bearers.

Below these were the higher functionaries, who ran the administration and ensured order throughout the country. These civil servants became more important particularly from the 5th Dynasty onwards. Their statues and tombs provide excellent testimony to the opulent life they led.

The scribes were another very important class. According to one papyrus document, this is *"the number one job and it is an honour to have it; the scribe takes*

■ Crowns and other symbols of the Pharaoh over the centuries.

note of the accounts for everything and on him depends the army."

Farmers and workers, the former busy in the fields, the latter in workshops, formed the base of the civilisation, as can be seen in representations of everyday life, and suffered from the most difficult conditions. The two groups are considered the most important factors in Egyptian civilisation, crucial to its size and importance.

Architecture

The history of architecture in Ancient Egypt begins with the discovery of adobe. The first temples, houses and tombs were made from adobe, wood and reeds. However, Imhotep, architect of the Pharaoh Djoser (2654-2635 BC), who built the Saqqara Step Pyramid, revolutionised construction techniques by using stone for the first time in Egypt.

Very little remains today of Ancient Egyptian **cities**, for the simple reason that all their constructions, including the Pharaoh's palace, were built using perishable materials (adobe, wood and reeds) and due to the custom of rebuilding houses once their structure became very deteriorated. Only in very rare cases were certain workers' villages actually abandoned.

Even today, excavation work cannot give us a very good idea of what an Old Kingdom city was really like. It would seem, however, that Memphis, the cap-

ital, was organised into residential areas containing palaces and houses for the ordinary people, all protected by a kind of fortress in a total area measuring 13 x 6.5 km². Crop fields and gardens were interspersed amongst these buildings.

Only one text is conserved to tell us what Itj-Tawy, the capital of the Middle Kingdom, looked like. It describes the site as a green rectangle, bordered on two sides by water and on the other two by the desert, but gives no details about the city itself. We know more about Kahun, a workers' village: it was formed by a 400 x 350 m rectangle protected by strong walls and divided internally into two parts by another wall. The houses of the richer inhabitants were on the east side of this, whilst the poor lived on the west side.

Two New Kingdom cities survive: the first of these, in Tell El-Amarna, is Akhetaten, the capital founded by Pharaoh Akhenaten; the second is Deir El-Medina, on the west bank of Thebes. Akhetaten stretches for some 9 km beside the Nile. In the centre, facing each other, are the Pharaoh's palace and the city's main temple, whilst scattered all around are noble villas, the houses of poorer citizens and the administrative buildings. Deir El-Medina is where the workers and artists who worked on the Valleys of the Kings, Queens

Palace of Menreptah in Memphis.

and Nobles lived. It is structured around a main street and is surrounded by several hills, which made it easier to protect.

In Ancient Egyptian cities, the **royal palace** was always situated in the centre, opposite the main temple. These were the two most important buildings in the city. Because of Egypt's hot climate, the royal palace, like the houses, was built of adobe and wood, as we can see from the ruins of the palace of Amenophis III in Malkata, "the west bank of Luxor", and those of Seti I in Abydos, Ramses II in Tanis, Menreptah in Memphis and Akhenaten in Tell El-Amarna. This last gives us the best idea of what a Pharaoh's palace was like: huge in size, protected by high walls, with an enormous garden full of palm and sycamore trees, and vast pools with lotus flowers. Inside, palaces were usually divided into two zones: the private area, containing the Pharaoh's residence and harem and the apartments of the princes and princesses; and the state area, with corridors, courtyards, administrative chambers and, above all, the Pharaoh's throne room. Nearly all royal palaces have a "window of appearances", opening onto the street, where the Pharaoh and his family would show themselves to the people, bestowing gifts of gold on the faithful.

Regarding **noble villas**, the scenes depicted on noblemen's tombs in Thebes and Tell El-Amarna show that they lived in houses whose structure imitated that of the Pharaoh's palace. These villas, which might be as large as a hectare in area, were, like the temples and royal palace, protected by walls. Inside was a garden leading to a columned reception area guarding a two-storey house. The apartments of the nobleman, his harem and his children were always on the upper floor, which had a north-facing terrace roof allowing the inhabitants to enjoy the fresh breeze in summer. The granaries, stores, kitchen, servants' quarters and stables were located in a corner of the garden, always south of the house so that unpleasant smells were carried away by the wind.

The **houses** of middle-class and working people had two or more storeys, built over the granary. The main fronts, normally not decorated, consisted of a projecting door supported by two columns with lintel. The work area was on the ground floor, whilst the owners' rooms were on the upper floor, with windows for natural lighting, often with curtains. Roofs were sometimes slightly inclined to drain off rainwater, a most unusual detail, as it rains very little in Egypt, but this was still something that Egyptian architects might take into account.

The remains of workers' houses can be seen in El Lahun and Deir El-Medina. In El-Lahun, the houses generally have four rooms, with a staircase leading to the roof. In Deir El-Medina, the most usual model also features four parts. In the first, the entrance to the house, stand jugs with water. From here, we enter the main room, which has a higher ceiling, supported in the centre by one or more columns.

■ Model of the houses used by workers and artists in Deir El-Medina.

In this room are adobe benches for visitors, and a dining table. In a niche in one corner is the statue of a god. The third room is the main bedroom, which opens at the end onto a yard for cooking and baking bread.

The earliest design for the **temple** was based on an open courtyard surrounded by a reed wall. A covered chapel was later added to this, providing the base for what, with time, would develop into the characteristic design of what we now know as the Egyptian temple. The temple is structured into several parts: an avenue of sphinxes leading to the main entrance, a pylon (from the Greek *pylos*, meaning gate) which forms the front, an open courtyard with a row of columns on either side providing entrance for nobles during festivities, a columned hypostyle hall reserved for the priests and princes, a smaller hall or antechamber where offerings were prepared and, at the end, the sanctuary, the holiest place in the temple, containing the statue of the god to which it is dedicated. All these elements are enclosed within adobe brick walls representing the first water and within which was a sacred lake from which water was taken for purification rites.

From what we can deduce from different depictions, when the construction of a temple began, the Pharaoh would make a hole in which the ten founding tablets were placed. These tablets were made of

Pylon at the Temple of Luxor. ■

different materials and were inscribed on either with the names of the Pharaoh or the god to which the temple was devoted. Once construction was complete, the Pharaoh would return to inaugurate the temple.

To build the pylon gateway, an adobe brick ramp was used to raise the stone blocks, which were dovetailed together. Once construction was complete, the blocks were cut to give the whole the same angle of inclination. This technique of inclin-

Open papyriform column. Courtyard of Amenophis III. Temple of Luxor. ■

■ **Temple of Esna:** columns with composite capitals in the hypostyle hall.

had the same diameter. Different types are found in different places in the country and at different periods: **fluted columns**, found for the first time in the Djoser enclosure (2654-2563 BC); **palmiform columns**, representing eight palm fronds lashed to a pole, and found from the 5th Dynasty on; **lotiform columns**, representing the lotus flower, the type most commonly used in the Old and Middle Kingdoms, as well as during the Graeco-Roman period; **papyriform columns**, also found from the 5th Dynasty on and the type most used in the New Kingdom, representing the papyrus plant in two ways, open and closed; **coniform columns**, which are found for the first time in the Djoser Step Pyramid wall but were little used subsequently; **tent pole columns**, being representations of the poles used to support the Pharaoh's campaign tent, an example of which we can see in the Festive Temple of Thutmosis III at Karnak; **Hathor columns**, first found in the Middle Kingdom and representing the goddess Hathor with the head and ears of a cow and the face of a woman; and **composite columns**, decorated with floral motifs and widely used during the Graeco-Roman period.

It would appear that the first **obelisks** were built in the city of Heliopolis, from where they spread all over Egypt. Obelisks symbolise Ra, the sun god, their pyramidal points designed to be the first and last to receive the sun's rays. They were normally built in pairs and placed at temple entrances as a gift to the gods to commemorate festivities, anniversaries or victories. Obelisks are made from a single block of stone, usually granite, and can weigh more than one hundred tons. They represent the clearest testimony to Ancient Egyptian advances in cutting and shaping hard stone.

The highest obelisks we can seen today are found in San Giovanni Square in Rome (32.18 m, built

ing the walls towards the interior made them more stable, and was used in almost all walls in Ancient Egypt.

The **columns** were built by burying the base in sand and using blocks that were later cut so that they all

■ **Types of column.**

| Fluted | Palmiform | Lotiform | Papyriform | Coniform | Tent pole | Composite | Hathor |

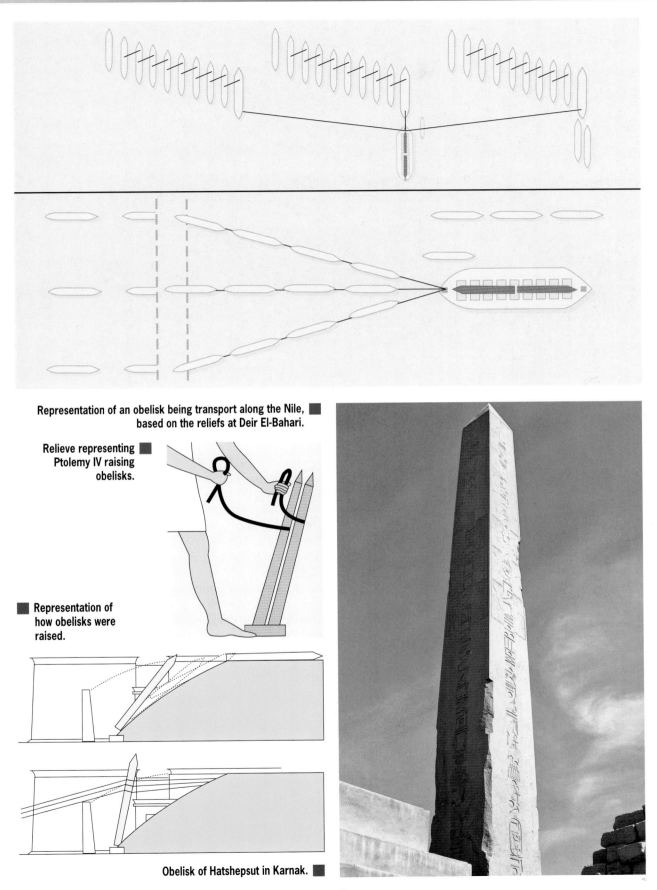

Representation of an obelisk being transport along the Nile, based on the reliefs at Deir El-Bahari.

Relieve representing Ptolemy IV raising obelisks.

Representation of how obelisks were raised.

Obelisk of Hatshepsut in Karnak.

■ The Step Pyramid in Saqqara.

■ Road leading from the temple in the valley to the mortuary Temple of Unas.

by Thutmosis III); in the temple at Karnak (29.56 m, built by Hatshepsut); in Atmeidan, Istanbul (28.95 m, built by Thutmosis III); in St Peter's Square in Rome (25.37 m, by an unknown Pharaoh); and in the temple at Luxor (25 m, built by Ramses II).

The earliest Ancient Egyptian **tombs** in the Ancient Egypt were simply pits in the ground covered by stones. Later, a vertical shaft was built to the funeral chamber, and the tomb was covered by a rectangular stone construction. These early designs, used to bury the first Pharaohs, are known as **mastabas** ("adobe bench" in Arabic).

During the early days of the 3rd Dynasty, Imhotep, Pharaoh Djoser's architect, began to build a stone

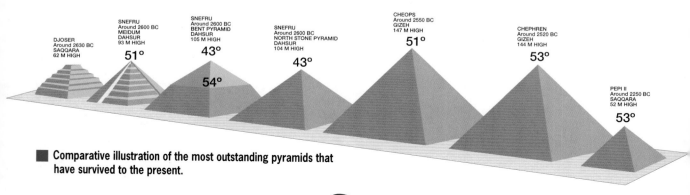

DJOSER
Around 2630 BC
SAQQARA
62 M HIGH

SNEFRU
Around 2600 BC
MEIDUM
DAHSUR
93 M HIGH
51°

SNEFRU
Around 2600 BC
BENT PYRAMID
DAHSUR
105 M HIGH
43°
54°

SNEFRU
Around 2600 BC
NORTH STONE PYRAMID
DAHSUR
104 M HIGH
43°

CHEOPS
Around 2550 BC
GIZEH
147 M HIGH
51°

CHEPHREN
Around 2520 BC
GIZEH
144 M HIGH
53°

PEPI II
Around 2250 BC
SAQQARA
52 M HIGH
53°

■ Comparative illustration of the most outstanding pyramids that have survived to the present.

mastaba, which finally took shape as the **Step Pyramid**, the first of its type. Subsequent Pharaohs were also buried in step pyramids until the reign of Sneferu, founder of the 4th Dynasty. When he came to the throne, Sneferu ordered the construction of what is now known as the Bent or Red Pyramid, the first perfect pyramid in history. Thanks to the experience accumulated during the times of his father, Sneferu, however, Cheops was the most fortunate Pharaoh, as his is the largest and most perfect of all. Cheops' son and grandson, Chephren and Mycerinus respectively, boast the other two most perfect pyramids in Egypt.

Later, the Pharaohs of the 5th Dynasty began to give more importance to the mortuary temple that was built beside the pyramid. The funeral chambers of Unas, last Pharaoh of the 5th Dynasty, and the 6th Dynasty Pharaohs contain the inscriptions known as the *Pyramid Texts* (see chapter on "What is there after death?").

In the times of the Middle Kingdom, the Pharaohs built adobe brick pyramids covered with stone, but this covering was lost over time, and many of them became little more than piles of mud. A total of 98 pyramids have been found from the thousand-year period covering the Old and Middle Empires, when they were built as the burial places of the Pharaohs, though most were sacked even during those times.

A mortuary temple was always built on the east side of the pyramid, and it was here that the priests carried out rites to help the Pharaoh return to life. The temple adjoined another, built lower down and known as the valley temple, which is where the priests purified and mummified the Pharaoh's body.

The Pharaohs of the New Kingdom ceased building pyramids and sought a distant site ("virgin", according to Innini, the architect of this first type of tomb): the **Valley of the Kings**. All the New Kingdom Pharaohs were buried here, and 62 tombs have been found to date. The last to be discovered, as well as the most important, was that of the famed Pharaoh Tutankhamun. His mortuary temples do not stand beside his tombs as was the custom, no doubt so as not to make it easy for tomb robbers to find the burial site. All these temples were built near the Nile Valley, on the west bank of Luxor, and those that have survived to our day provide testimony to the wealth and grandeur of Egypt in those times, as in earlier periods.

Temple of Medinet Habu in Luxor. ■

Turning now to the **tombs of the nobles**, during the times when the Pharaohs built pyramids, noblemen built their own tombs in the form of mastabas, with a vertical shaft and a structure above, divided into different chambers and chapels. Under the New Kingdom, the nobles reached the very mountain where the Pharaohs built their tombs. During this period, noble tombs consisted of two chapels forming an inverted "T" shape, with a vertical shaft connecting to the exterior, leading to the funeral chamber.

During the times of the Pharaohs, ordinary people were buried in very simple tombs, mere pits made in the ground, and very little in the way of personal belongings were left in these graves.

■ Illustrations in the Tomb of Tutankhamun: mask of the Pharaoh, the tomb as it was found, with all the original furnishings, and the four sarcophagi (one inside the other) where the Pharaoh's body was laid to rest.

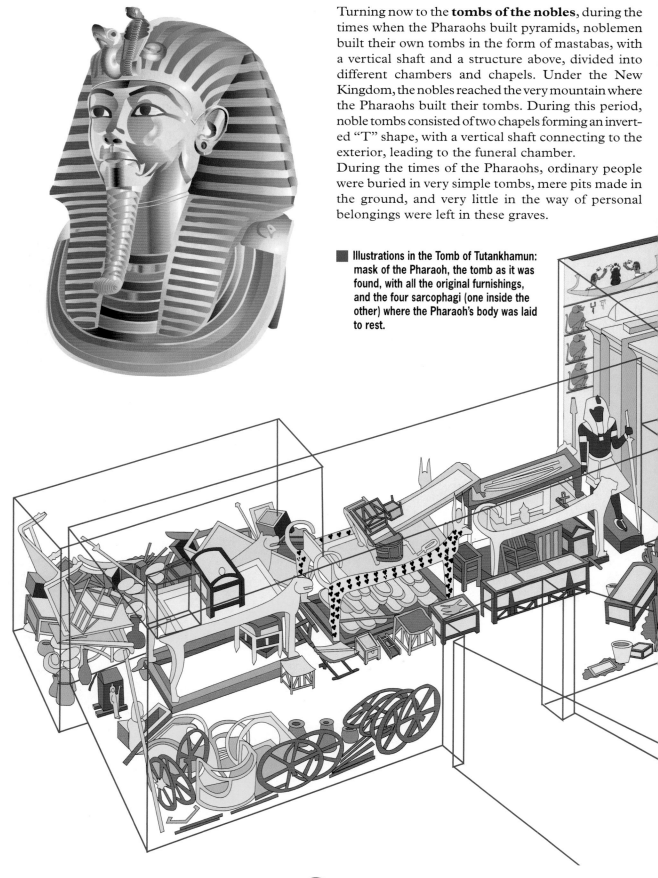

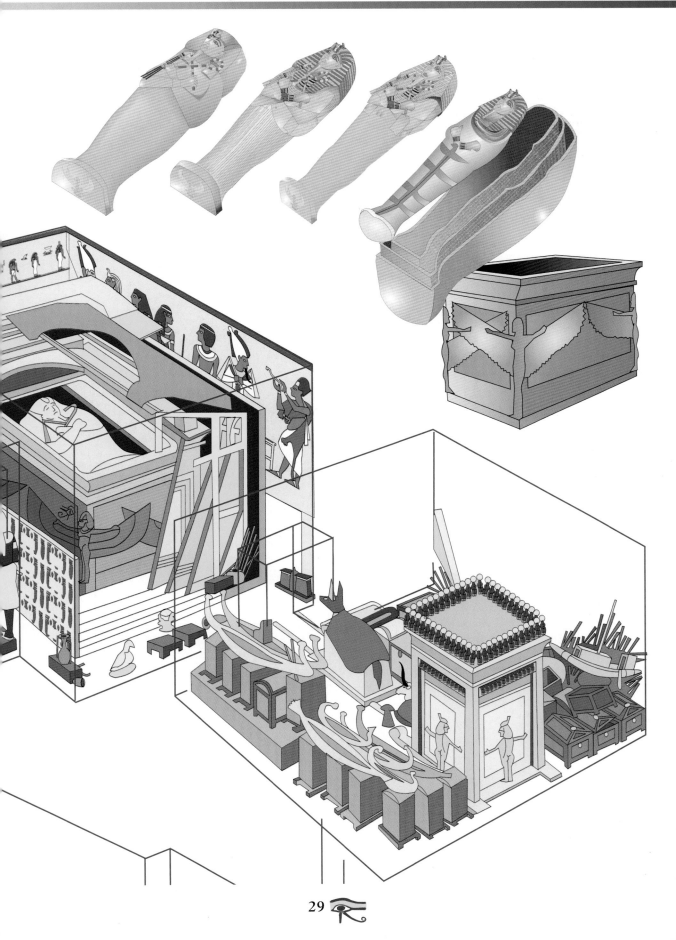

Art

Egyptian art possesses a very special quality: it never appears shocking or strange to us; on the contrary, it is universally appreciated and admired. The first Egyptian artists were active in prehistoric times, painting earthenware pots, forming reliefs on the palettes they used to grind their colours, and making clay sculptures. Little by little, in around 3000 BC, a style became defined.

Egyptian mythology exercised considerable control over art or, to put it another way, art was used as a vehicle for mythology. The materials used were soft stones such as limestone, hard stones like granite and diorite, wood and metal. Egyptian artists carved statues that closely resembled the people they were portraying in order to breathe life into them and help the soul recognise the dead person on its return. For this reason, considerable importance was attached to the gaze, and these statues were often encrusted with glass eyes. In reliefs and paintings, the human face is always shown in profile, the eye and shoulders face on, the rest of the body in profile in order to show the most characteristic features of the subject to the full.

Themes other than human figures are always represented from strange perspectives. For example, objects on tables are depicted as if observed from above, whilst the sacks carried by a donkey are drawn one on top of another in order to represent both.

Although Egyptian civilisation has bequeathed us some fine examples of painting, relieves, both bas-reliefs and haut-reliefs, are much more abundantly found. They were made directly on the stone used for construction and, if no suitable stone was available, as in the case of the tombs in the Valley of the Kings, the walls were previously covered with a layer of plas-

■ Terracotta Naqada II Period jar, decorated with primitive painting. Egyptian Museum of Cairo.

Head found at Merimdet ■ Beni Salama.

Reliefs on the tomb of Ramose, Luxor. ■

■ Illustration on the four steps to creating a relief in Ancient Egypt.

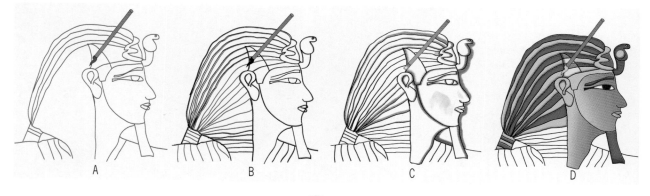

A   B   C   D

ter. The procedure for executing a relief was as follows: first a grid was drawn to render the proportions, then the figures were drawn using red ink, and corrected using black ink. Next, the specialists arrived with their hammers and chisels to make the reliefs and, finally, these were coloured.

The pigments used were of mineral origin. The raw material was ground and mixed with water, then applied to the walls, which absorbed this substance, for which reason the colours of many monuments have been conserved over the years. Blue was made from copper carbonate, green from powdered malachite, red and yellow from different iron oxides, black from carbon and white from lime. A wider range could be obtained by mixing two or more colours.

Writing

Writing is a constant feature of Egyptian art, the most characteristic form being hieroglyphics, a word deriving from the Greek *hieros glyfos*, meaning "sacred engravings". Hieroglyphics are used to decorate temples and tombs, as well as to identify statues of gods or the subjects by their name and attributes so that, later, the ritual of "opening the mouth" will help the soul to recognise its master.

The texts that accompany scenes in the temples are repetitive formulas describing how the Pharaoh makes an offering to a god and how this god praises the Pharaoh for his works. They are more varied in the tombs, where they accompany scenes from everyday life and tell us about many aspects of it, such as farming, industry, sport, festivities, etc. Other texts accompany funeral scenes, and tell us about the rites performed for the dead, and the journey to the other world.

A simpler form of writing emerged in the 5th Dynasty; hieratic ("priestly") writing, used principally on papyruses. It consists of abbreviated forms of the same hieroglyphics, written more quickly using pen and ink. A third form of writing, demotic ("public script") was used from the 25th Dynasty on. This was similar to hieratic but with fewer details. With the arrival of the Greeks, the Egyptians started to use the Greek alphabet, from which Coptic script was developed.

It was Jean-François Champollion who took the most important steps towards deciphering hieroglyphic writing through his studies of the famous Rosetta Stone, which was discovered in 1799. The inscription on it is a priestly document thanking Ptolemy V for opening up the temples to the ordinary people for the first time in history, and is written in three languages: hieroglyphics, Egyptian demotic and Greek. Other philologists continued the work until, in the early-20th century, the grammar and vocabulary of these scripts had been completely deciphered.

Hieroglyphics are a mixture of pictograms and ideograms, divided into alphabets, biliteral (two-letter) and triliteral (three-letter) signs and determinatives. They may be written from left to right, from right to left or in vertical columns.

Examples of hieroglyphic writing. ■

EGYPTIAN ALPHABET:

Example of bilateral signs:

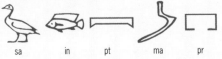

sa   in   pt   ma   pr

Example of trilateral signs:

nfr   anj(kh)   jnt   Asha

■ Temple of Denderah: the god Bes.

Religion

The Ancient Egyptians believed that, in the beginning, the world was covered in water, from which the first god, the creator, Atum-Ra, emerged in Heliopolis. Atum-Ra, the sun god, created Shu, the air god, and Tefnut, goddess of atmospheric moisture. Shu and Tefnut begat Geb, god of the earth, and Nut, goddess of the sky, and these had four children: two males, Osiris and Set, and two females, Isis and Nephthys. In the religion of Memphis, Ptah created the world merely by thinking and saying so.

The oldest known religious texts, known as the "Pyramid Texts" (circa 2500 BC), speak of a multitude of deities, some of them local and only worshipped in their particular territories, others adored throughout the country. All were given a human aspect, and triads (divine father, mother and child) were formed for each city. Since each was also given an animal characteristic related to their attributes, the gods were represented as having at once human and animal form. The deities were worshipped in their respective temples, which were, we remember, the only stone build-

Partial view of the sculpture of Hathor. Egyptian Museum of Cairo. ■

ings in the city. The priests kept the ordinary people in ignorance and obscurity as they conducted their worship of the gods, prohibiting them from entering the temples. Only the priests could enter, and even then there were categories. The high priest of the temple was, like the Pharaoh, the only one who could enter the sanctuary every morning to carry out the daily ritual. This consisted of approaching the tabernacle where the gold statue of the god was kept, taking it out to wash it and perfume it, burning incense, then depositing offerings before it. The priest then walked backwards out of the chamber, erasing his footprints from the ground, finally closing the sanctuary doors once more. The common people were completely excluded from all this, and were only allowed to see the sacred barque on which the priests carried the statue of the god during festivities and celebrations, otherwise taking the priests' word for everything.

Myths form an important part of Egyptian religion, particularly the myth of Isis and Osiris, according to which, Set was jealous of his brother Osiris. One day, Set slipped unseen into the palace of Osiris whilst his brother was sleeping, and measured his body. He then

■ Fragment from the Pyramid Texts. Pyramid of Unas.

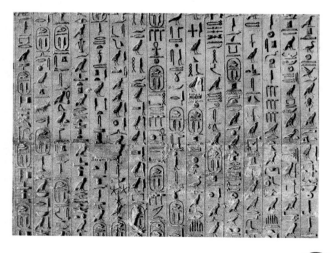

The Pharaoh carrying out rituals before the statue of Amun. ■

made a gold chest exactly to his brother's measurements and held a feast, promising that whoever could fit exactly into the chest should keep it. When Osiris got in to try it for size, Set's servants locked it and threw it into the Nile. Isis then went in search of her husband's body. Near the Nile, a tear fell from her face, causing the river to flood. She eventually found the chest, returned her husband to life and slept with him. But Set's servants found and killed her husband again, this time cutting his body into 14 pieces and scattering them all over the country. Isis set out to search for Osiris once more, accompanied this time by her sister, Nephthys. Taking the form of vultures, the sisters found all the pieces of Osiris' body except one, wrapping them in linen bandages. Isis gave birth to a son, Horus, who grew up and sought vengeance for his father's death, waging war on his uncle. In the end, the gods decided to judge the two rivals, making Osiris king of the other world and Horus the king of earth, but banishing Set into the desert, far from the fertile lands.

Amulets, used since prehistoric times, were very important to the ancient Egyptians. Various types existed: the Ankh, or key of life to a long and eternal life, the scarab beetle for luck and eternity, the Djed pillar for stability, the girdle of Isis for protection, the Was zsceptre for prosperity and the eye of Horus, which was an amulet giving strength, protection, safety and health. Symbolism was also contained in the materials used to make the amulet: gold, the same colour as the sun, signifies eternity or continuation; dark blue lapis lazuli

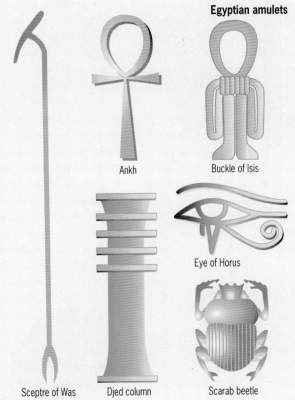

Egyptian amulets

Ankh

Buckle of Isis

Eye of Horus

Sceptre of Was

Djed column

Scarab beetle

symbolises the primeval water in which the whole world was submerged, and from which the first god emerged to create life; blue-green turquoise, water of the annual flooding of the Nile, bringing life to Egypt; whilst scarlet symbolises blood, the vital liquid for life.

Atum

Osiris

Amun

Min

Ptah
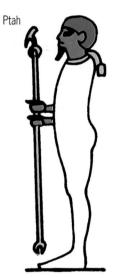

Khonsu

Bes

Mut

Maat

Selkis

Hathor

Isis

Nephthys

Nile

Sekhmet/Tefnut

Anubis

Anubis

Khnum

Thoth

Horus

Ra

Sobek

Aten

What is there after death?

For the Ancient Egyptians, the Nile represented the line dividing life from death. People lived on the east bank, where the sun rises, whilst the dead were buried on the west bank. Death was the transition from the first life to eternal life, so when someone died, their body was taken to the other side of the river, where the funeral rites were carried out on it. This consisted, firstly, of washing the body in pure Nile water, using aromatic elements such as soap, burning incense to complete the purification process.

The second ritual was mummification, a process which,

■ Purification of the dead. Tomb of Petosiris, Tuna El-Gebel.

in the case of the Pharaohs, took around 70 days to complete. For the first 40 days, the body lay on an inclined table, covered with balls of salt known as natron, which were changed every day. At the end of this 40-day period, the body was completely dry. Next, a incision was made in the left-side of the body in order to remove the internal organs (stomach, intestines, liver and lungs), which were kept in the so called Canopic jars. The abdomen was then treated with aromatic resins and stuffed with linen, after which the incision was sewn up again. Finally, the body was wrapped in linen strips or bandages and covered in pitch to isolate the body completely.

The third ritual was known as "opening the mouth". The high priest touched the body with a wooden adze, as if opening the mouth, nose, ears and eyes, thus enabling the deceased to communicate with the external world.

Once the funeral rites were completed, the priests and family members came to make offerings to call back the soul of the deceased to rejoin the body once more and enjoy eternal life. To this end, the body was buried with everything that might be useful to him in the other life: food, drink, jewellery and furniture. All this was carried to the tomb in a funeral procession led by the deceased's eldest son and accompa-

nied till the door of the tomb by other relatives and weeping mourners. The procession was completed by the sarcophagus, the Canopic jars and the funeral equipments.

People in Ancient Egypt greatly feared the path that

Offering carriers. Tomb of Ptah-Hotep (25th century BC). ■

Scene from a funeral procession, with the weeping mourners ■ in the centre. Tomb of Ramose, Luxor.

had to be taken in order to reach the other life and eternal happiness, as this was a dark, dangerous route plagued by devils and enemies trying to confuse the dead spirits and cause them to lose their way. The texts and drawings that decorated tomb walls were designed to help the deceased to avoid the dangers of the journey. These are the so-called *Pyramid Texts*, which are found in the 5th and 6th Dynasty pyramids, and which contain nearly 3,000 hymns. The common people began to use the same texts during the Middle Kingdom, though with slight changes. However, as they were not buried in pyramids, these texts were written inside the sarcophagi, and are known as the *Sarcophagi Texts*. In the New Kingdom, they were replaced by the *Book of the Dead*, made up of similar texts, but written on a papyrus scroll placed next to the body. This was, then, a cheaper and more practical way than writing them on the sarcophagi. In the tombs in the Valley of the Kings, we find scenes accompanied by texts describing the other world in

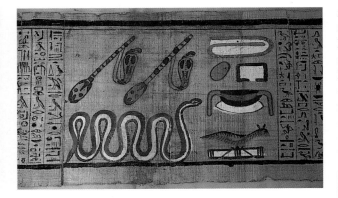

"Book of the Dead". Egyptian Museum of Cairo.

ment, which also appears in the *Book of the Dead*. In it, Osiris is portrayed as the great judge, whilst behind him are his sisters, Isis and Nephthys, and before him is Horus, presenting the deceased to Osiris. Beside him is Thoth, who carries scales containing the deceased's heart on one side and on the other the feather, symbol of justice. Beside the scales is Amam, an animal with the head of a crocodile and the body of a hippopotamus. If the deceased's heart should weigh more than the feather, Amam will eat it.

Horus weighing the heart of the deceased. This is a key scene in both the "Book of the Dead" and the "Book of Doors". The painting is from the tomb of the noble Menna in Luxor.

Ancient Egyptian eyes. In several different versions, they show the Pharaoh accompanying the sun god on his journey through the night until the sun rises once more the next day. These include the reliefs and texts in the *Book of Hidden Chambers* (Amduat), found in the tombs of Thutmose III, Amenophis II, Seti I and Ramses III. The book is divided into twelve parts, representing the twelve hours of the night. In turn, each part is divided into three registers: Ra appears in the central register passing to the other world in his sacred barque and observing how both the good and the bad are treated. The seventh hour of the book depicts the confrontation between the light and order represented by Ra with the darkness and chaos symbolised by Apophis, a giant serpent standing at the prow of the solar barque, with knives in his body, following the sun until it rises once more.

Another traditional book, similar to the previous one, is the *Book of Gates*. This book is also divided into twelve parts, each with three registers. The title is an allusion to the fact that at the beginning of each part is a door guarded by a vertical serpent. Parts of this book are reproduced in 19th and 20th Dynasty tombs. The most important scene is that of the final judge-

The representation of the goddess Nut on the ceiling of several funeral chambers in the Valley of the Kings is also very interesting. The Ancient Egyptians considered Nut, sky goddess the mother of the god Ra. She is seen arching over the earth, supported by her arms. In the morning, she gives birth to the sun, which emerges from between her legs and passes over her body, reaching her mouth at the end of the day. When night falls, the goddess Nut swallows the sun disk, which travels through her body throughout the night, only to be "reborn" in the same way the next morning.

Paintings from the "Book of Doors".
Tomb of Seti I, Luxor.

Representation of the goddess Nut on the ceiling of the funeral chamber of Ramses VI in Luxor.

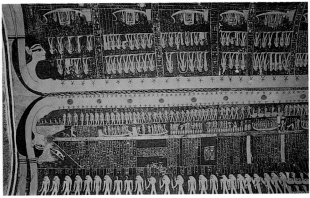

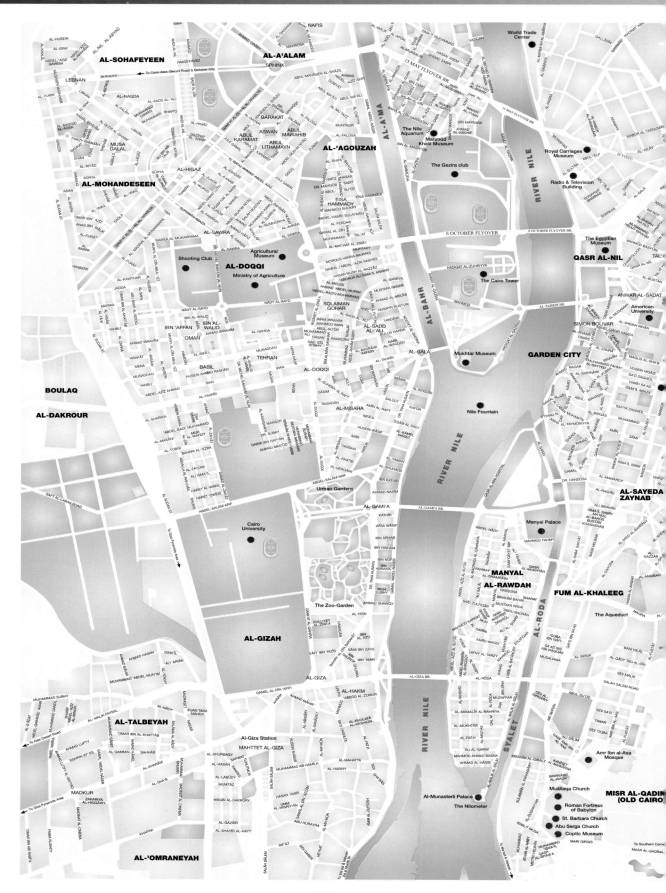

CAIRO

Cairo, seen from the Nile.

Amr Ibn Al-Ass, the leader of the Arab conquest, ordered the construction of the first Arab city in Egypt, El-Fustat (which means tent), as the capital of the new state of the Muslim caliphate in the year 641. In the 9th century, Ibn Tulun established the first autonomous Muslim state of Egypt and ordered the construction of another capital a little to the north of El-Fustat, which he called Al-Qatai. After the arrival of the Fatimids in Egypt, the leader of its army, Jawhar Al-Sequely, erected a royal residence in the year 969, which he called Al-Qahira ("overcoming"), which the name Cairo is derived from. In 1176, when Saladin began to govern Egypt, he united that royal residence with the preceding cities (El-Fustat and Al-Qatai) and called all of them together Cairo. Cairo, under the rule of the Mamelukes from the 13th century on, became the most important city in the world and the centre of Islamic art. For this reason, the Ottomans, when they arrived in 1543, took most of the city's architects, artisans and artists to Istanbul in order to make it just as beautiful as Cairo. Today Cairo is one of the largest cities in the world, especially Greater Cairo, which includes the provinces of Giza and Al-Qaliobeya, with a population that reaches 17 million inhabitants.

Modern Cairo

Midan Al-Tahrir (Liberation Square) is the main square of Cairo. Here, the central offices of the main airline companies, various hotels and travel agencies are concentrated. But the most important building is the **Egyptian Museum of Cairo**, born from the idea of the Frenchman Mariette in 1858. Its construction, however, wasn't completed until December 8, 1902.

Midan Al-Tahrir in the 1920s. ■

Midan Al-Tahrir (Liberation Square).

Front and interior of the Egyptian Museum of Cairo.

The **Egyptian Museum of Cairo** possesses more than 120,000 pieces, divided between two floors. On the first, stone monuments are exhibited in chronological order, beginning with the **palette of Narmer** (31st century BC), which commemorates the unification of the North and the South. The Pharaoh is represented on both sides of the palette, on one with the Southern Crown killing the northern monarch with his mace, and on the other, the Northern Crown parading in celebration of its victory (room 43). Other noteworthy

The Narmer palette.

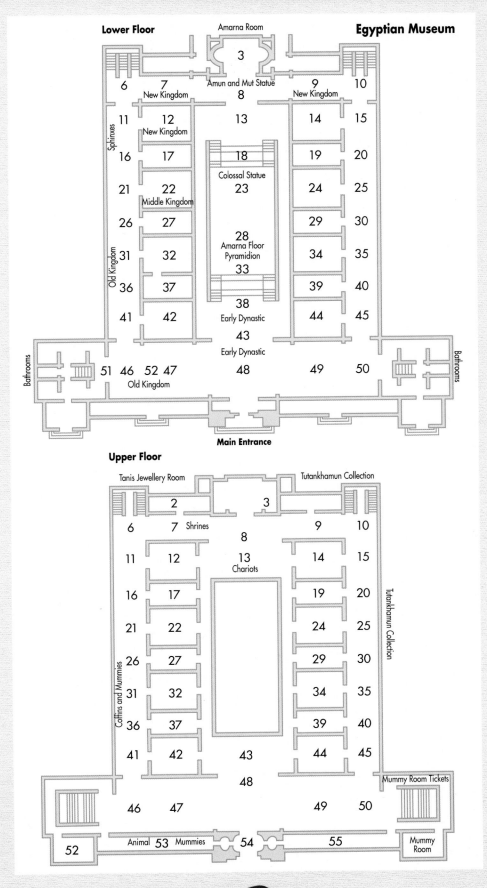

Lower Floor

Amarna Room

Egyptian Museum

3

Amun and Mut Statue

6   7   8   9   10
New Kingdom   New Kingdom

Sphinxes

11   12   13   14   15
New Kingdom

16   17   18   19   20
Colossal Statue

21   22   23   24   25
Middle Kingdom

26   27   28   29   30
Amarna Floor
Pyramidion

Old Kingdom

31   32   33   34   35

36   37   38   39   40
Early Dynastic

41   42   43   44   45
Early Dynastic

Bathrooms   Bathrooms

51 46 52 47   48   49   50
Old Kingdom

Main Entrance

Upper Floor

Tanis Jewellery Room   Tutankhamun Collection

2   3

6   7   Shrines   9   10

8

11   12   13   14   15
Chariots

Tutankhamun Collection

16   17   19   20

21   22   24   25

Coffins and Mummies

26   27   29   30

31   32   34   35

36   37   39   40

41   42   43   44   45

48

Mummy Room Tickets

46   47   49   50

52   Animal 53 Mummies   54   55   Mummy Room

The figures from Mycerinus: the goddess Hathor (right), Mycerinus (centre), and a local deity from Thebes (left).

pieces are those of **Mycerinus** (26th century BC), carved in highly polished basalt. These three pieces represent Mycerinus, the goddess Hathor and a local divinity, respectively (room 47).

The sculptural masterpieces from the Old Kingdom (from the 27th to the 23rd century BC) are found in rooms 42 and 32. In room 42, the seated scribe and the statues of Chephren and the Mayor, and in 32, the statues of Rahotep and Nofret and the fresco of the geese of Maidum. About the **seated scribe**, a work carved in coloured limestone, the most outstanding feature is the expressive look in the eyes, inlaid with crystal, which reflects his attention to what he is going to write on the roll of papyrus on his lap. The **statuette of Chephren** (26th century BC), carved in diorite, the second hardest material in the world, represents Chephren seated on his throne with the god Horus in the form of a falcon behind his head. The **statue of the Mayor** (Cheikh el Beled),

■ The sitting scribe.

■ La statue of Chephren.

La statue of the Mayor ■ (Cheikh El Beled).

Statues of Rahotep and ■ Nofret.

Statuette of Cheops.

■ **Statue of Tuthmosis III.**

carved in sycamore wood and also with inlaid eyes, is a life-size representation of this priest, a little chubby and bald. The **statues of Rahotep and Nofret**, carved in painted limestone, represent a brother of Cheops with a moustache, and his wife in her transparent dress. The eyes are marvellously inlaid. About the **fresco of the geese of Maidum** (26th century BC), the perfectly preserved polychrome and the details shown in these birds are particularly noteworthy. From room 32, we enter room 37, which exhibits a part of the funerary furniture of Queen **Hetepheres**, the mother

The geese of Maidum. ■

of Cheops (27th century BC), including her sarcophagus, her viscera and her furniture. You can also admire the only statue of **Cheops** in existence here. It is a small piece carved in ivory.

Likewise, a visit to rooms 11 and 12, containing works from the New Kingdom, is recommended, as they feature magnificent statues like those of **Thutmose III** (15th century BC), especially the small one

■ Head of Nefertiti.

Sculpture of the goddess Hathor con Amenophis II. ■

carved in marble that shows him on his knees offering wine to the Gods; and the chapel and statue of the goddess Hathor in the form of a cow with **Amenhotep II**, found in and brought from Thebes. The **Akhenaten** room, number 3 is just as interesting due to the sculptures of this Pharaoh and, above all, the unfinished head of his wife **Nefertiti**.

Staircase number 6 leads us to the second floor. A large part of it is occupied by the funerary furniture of **Tutankhamun**, which was discovered by Carter on November 5, 1922 in his tomb in the Valley of the Kings, where his mommy still lies. The funerary equipment includes chapels, war chariots, bows, arrows, clothes, beds, chairs, statues, alabaster glasses, etc. The Pharaoh's treasure is exhibited in room 3 and it includes his gold mask, two of his three coffins, one of solid gold and the other of gilded wood, and the

Funerary items of Tutankhamun: funeral chapel and canopic jars.

Tutankhamun gold mask. ■

Tutankhamun's gold coffin.

Funerary objects of Tutankhamun: view of the throne and canopic chest.

■ Large gilt wooden box with statue of a jackal, representing the god Anubis, part of Tutankhamun's Treasure.

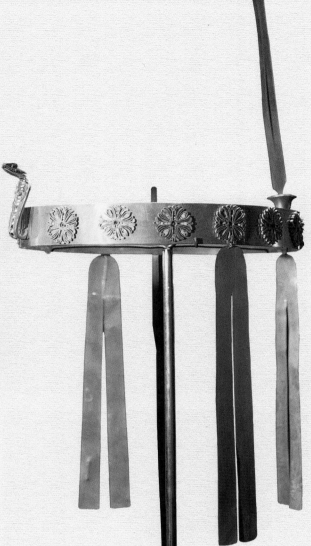

Crown of Sat-Hathor-Iwnet (12th Dynasty) and Roman period ■ necklace.

rest of his jewels. In the next room, the jewels from the entire Pharaonic era since the 32nd century BC are displayed, among which the bracelets of King Djer (1rst Dynasty) and the necklaces of the princesses from the Middle Kingdom stand out.

The room of the **royal mummies** is also found on the second floor, with mummies of such famous Pharaohs as Ramses II, Amenhotep II and Thutmose IV. This last one attracts a lot of attention due to the conservation of his hair, eyebrows and eyelashes.

Mummy of Ramses II. ■

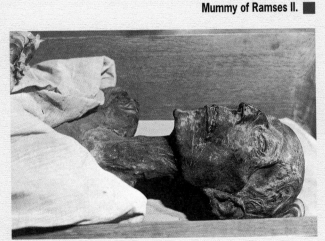

■ Opera square, in the present day and in the 1920s.

All around the museum are the streets that form the city centre, such **Talat Harb, Kasr el Nil, Ramses** and **el Tahrir**. These lead to **Talat Harb, Opera** and **Ramses squares**, with their restaurants, cinemas, banks and clothes and shoe shops.

The **Cairo Tower** is, at 187 m, the highest building in the country. It stands on a lotus-flower-shaped island in the Nile, and can be seen from practically any point in the city.

■ The Cairo Tower.

Amr Ibn Al-Ass Mosque: courtyard and entrance. ■

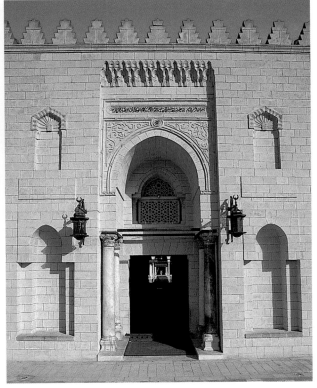

Islamic Cairo

Amr Ibn El-As ordered the construction of Cairo's first Islamic city, **El-Fustat**, near the old Roman fortress. The ruins of this city, which can still be visited, also contain the mosque that bears his name. **Amr Ibn El-As Mosque**, though it has since undergone much alteration and reconstruc-

Ibn Tulun Mosque. ■

■ Al-Azhar Mosque.

tion, was the first to be built in Egypt and in Africa.

Ibn Tulun Mosque, the largest and second oldest in Cairo, was built using columns of brick and stucco between the years 876 and 879 AD. It possesses a large open court and four porticoes, whose size and simplicity are surprising. In the centre was the fountain of ablutions under a dome. A minaret with a spiral shape is noteworthy, influenced by the architecture of Samarkand (Iraq), home of Ibn Tulun.

The Islamic Centre

Al-Azhar street divides the Islamic centre into two parts, the North and the South. On this street, stands the **Al-Azhar Mosque,** the main one in Cairo, built in the year 970 and which, in 988, Caliph Al-Aziz turned into the leading university in the world, where every kind of science, besides the Islamic religion, was taught. And so it continues, although the university has been moved to a larger building in another part of the city. It is an interesting work of architecture, which presents a mix of various styles, as can

Khan Al-Khalili Bazaar. ■

be observed in its distinct and marvellous minarets. The classes are not open to the public but the mosque is. Visitors are informed that entrance is free to all the mosques in Cairo. Behind the main entrance, we enter an upper court with a magnificent marble floor that leads to the main hall of the mosque, with its 140 columns. Men enter through the main door, whilst women, who have to keep their body and hair covered, enter through a side door to the right.

On the other side of Al-Azhar Street stretches the large bazaar of Cairo, **Khan Al-Khalili**, popular with tourists, who often shop here, especially for the variety of artisan crafts. During the Medieval Age, the Khan was a place where merchants lodged, kept their goods and rested their camels and horses. The name Khalili derives from Jaharkas Al-Khalil, the Prince who ordered the construction of this Khan in 1382. In 1511, Sultan El-Ghuri ordered it rebuilt as a commercial area. Here, as travellers described at the time, the best silk and pearls were sold. From this era, an arch called **Bab Al-Badistan** still stands, visible from one of the streets that give entry to the bazaar.

Bab Al-Badistan.

Bayt Al-Sohaimy.

El-Fishawy Café.

More than a market, Khan Al-Khalili is an area with lots of atmosphere, especially on summer nights, when many Cairoans come to its numerous sidewalk cafés. One of the oldest and most famous cafés is **El-Fishawy**, characteristic for its mirrors, where the Egyptian and Nobel Prize writer Naguib Mahfouz, who was from this area, was a frequent customer. He often wrote or was inspired here.

North of Jan El-Jalili, **al Muez street** is like an open-air museum of Islamic architecture. Here, we can see pretty mosques like that of **Sultan Qalawun**, whose mausoleum imitates the Dome of the Rock in Jerusalem, and that of **Nasser Mohammed**. The house called **Bayt Al-Sohaimy,** residence of the Sheikh of the Al-Azhar area in the 17th century, is also on this street. Today, after being restored by the government, it joins two other adjacent houses, also built in the 17th century, which belonged to El-Khauarazmy and Gafar. The three houses give a very good idea of what homes were like during the Islamic era.

The **walls** and gates that surround Cairo to the north are found at the end of al Muez street. They were built by Gawhar El-Sequely in the year 970 and rebuilt by Saladin in 1087. The two gates that are conserved in this area are called **Bab Al-Futuh** (Gate of Conquest) and **Bab El-Nasr** (Gate of Victory). Both, with two towers and very narrow windows, are good examples of military architecture during medieval times. Likewise, many inscriptions from the time of Napoleon's military campaign in Egypt in 1798 can be seen on both gates. There, where Al-Azhar and Al-Mu'ezz streets intersect, a few metres from the Al-Azhar Mosque, at the beginning of the 16th century, Sultan El-Ghuri ordered various buildings constructed, such as his wekala, a place where merchants lodged and stored their goods during their travels, his mosque-madrasa

■ Bab El-Futuh (Gate of Conquest).

Bab Al-Nasr (Gate of Victory). ■

(school) and his house. Known today as **Kasr El-Ghuri**, it has been transformed into a theatre where **Tanura** dancers perform their Sufi dances, in an extraordinary show, free on Saturdays, Mondays and Wednesdays, at 7 p.m. in the winter and 8 p.m. in the summer, organised by the Department of Culture. Currently, since the mosque is under reconstruction, the show takes place in the Citadel.

Continuing south along the street Al-Mu'ezz, we see

■ Sufi Tanura dancer.

Bab Zuela. ■

various old buildings and an interesting little market. And at the end stands another of the original gates of Cairo, **Bab Zuwela**, which together with Bab El-Nasr and Bab El-Futuh are the only three that are conserved from the 16 which originally enclosed the city. In 1415, El-Muaeyd Sheikh built two minarets in his mosque above the towers of Bab Zuwela, situated next to the gate and in which are two magnificent copper-lined wooden doors that originally belonged to the mosque of Sultan Hassan.

■ Various objects found in the Museum of Islamic Art: lamp, plate, jar, wooden door, astrolabe and prayer mat.

The **Museum of Islamic Art** is housed in a beautiful building, formerly Cairo's main library, known as Dar el Kutub, and which has now been relocated elsewhere in the city. The Museum of Islamic Art contains nearly 80,000 pieces that are displayed according to their material: in rooms 6 to 10, there are wooden pieces, with examples of marvellously carved and inlaid doors and pulpits; in room 11, metal objects, like candelabras, pitchers and astrolabes; in room 12, weapons and shields; in rooms 13 to 16, ceramic pieces representing different periods, techniques and schools; in room 19, manuscripts are displayed and in room 20, glass pieces. Moreover, almost all the museum walls are decorated with rugs, forming a really interesting collection.

■ Khanqah Barquq.

El-Darrasa was a favourite site for the Mamelukes kings (who governed Egypt from the 13th to the 16th centuries) to build their mausoleums or funeral complexes. Very good examples can still be seen today, such as the **Khanqah Barquq**, built by Sultan Farrag between 1400 and 1411, and the **mausoleum of Sultan Qaitbay**, built in 1472, an important work of 15th-century Islamic art and architecture. It includes a mosque, with a ceiling and stained glass window that still conserves its colour, a fountain for treating and cooling water, a Koran school and the mausoleum. Over time, homeless Cairoans and immigrants from the country, as well as refugees from the Suez Canal during the wars have installed themselves here, living next to the tombs where the dead continue to be buried, forming an incredible mixture of luxury buildings, tombs and houses. For this reason, this area is known as the **City of the Dead**.

The construction of the **Citadel** (or Alcala, in Arabic) was initiated in 1176 by Saladin and concluded in

■ The City of the Dead.

Qaitbay Mosque:
exterior and
interior.

Alabaster or Mohammed Ali Mosque: exterior and interior. ■

■ Qasr Al-Gawhara Palace: throne of Mohammed Ali and furniture of the French Empress Eugenia.

1207, on a hilltop of Al-Mukatam between Cairo and Fustat, in order to dominate both cities, after uniting them with high wall, which is said to have been made by fallen stones from the Great Pyramid. Since then and over many centuries, the Citadel was the residence of the Sultan of Egypt. The last king who lived in it was Mohammed Ali (1805-1848). The walls and towers of the Citadel constitute a good example of military architecture in medieval times in the Middle East.

Inside, the Citadel is occupied by various buildings. The **El-Nasser Mohammed Mosque**, built between 1318 and 1335, follows the usual model. In it, an open court with four porticoes supported by columns coming from previous temples of Pharaonic and Roman styles, the two minarets and a dome, covered with green ceramics, stand out. Inlays of different coloured marble and nacre are still preserved. The **Military Museum** and the **Police Museum**, apart from their contents, the second one offers a terrace with a magnificent panoramic view of the entire city, especially Saladin Square, where the main entrance of the Citadel is situated.

Qasr Al-Gawhara ("Jewel") is part of the palace where Mohammed Ali lived. His throne and some furniture are conserved here, along with portraits of the kings that succeeded him until Farouk, the last king of Egypt. Other interesting features include the bed and the furniture specially made for the French Empress Eugenia, brought from the palace, which was later turned into the Hotel Marriott.

The **Alabaster Mosque (or Mohammed Ali Mosque)** is the most elaborate mosque in Cairo. Its construction was initiated in 1824, in Ottoman style, just like the mosques in Istanbul. It consists of two parts: an open-air court with an alabaster fountain in the centre and a clock tower, a gift from the French king Louis Philip in 1846 in exchange for the obelisk of Ramses II, which stood at the door of the temple in Luxor and which now presides over Concord Square in Paris. The prayer hall is covered by a large, central dome, four semi-domes and four smaller domes that

■ The Sultan Hassan Mosque and, on the right, the Al-Rifai Mosque.

■ The Sultan Hassan Mosque: courtyard of ablutions and imam before the Mihrab.

display beautiful decorations. To the right, the tomb of Mohammed Ali is found. The two minarets of the mosque stretch 83 metres high and reach the heavens, as Mohammed Ali wished, "playing with the clouds".

Opposite the Citadel, the **square of Saladin (Salah Al-Din)** opens up. Two impressive mosques preside over the site. One is the **Mosque-Madrasa of Sultan Hassan**, a masterpiece of Islamic architecture, built between 1356 and 1362, which served as mosque, school, university city and mausoleum. The spectacular façade with its exquisite decoration formed with stalactites and geometric and floral motifs cannot fail to impress the visitor. After this, we enter a small room, where we leave our shoes, and then continue to what were the student rooms, distributed among various floors. Next, we reach the open court of the mosque, whose floor is covered with marble of different colours. In the centre, there is the fountain of ablutions, which is covered by a wooden dome. Four doors give access to the classrooms, where the four different rites of the Islamic religion were taught. Inside the mosque, there is the Mihrab (niche) oriented towards Mecca, and next to it, a pulpit for giving sermons, both carved in stone. Past the wall of the Mihrab, we reach the mausoleum, with a high dome and decorations such as stalactite colouring in the corners.

Sultan Hassan is not buried here, but his son, since the body of the sultan was lost in battle.

The other great mosque in Saladin Square is the **Al-Rifai Mosque**. It was built by Queen Dawlat Juchiar, the mother of Ismail, after 1869. Entering it, to the right, we can admire beautiful elements of Islamic decoration, and, to the left, the tombs of the two last Egyptian kings, Fouad and Farouk, and of the last Shah of Persia, Reza Bahlawy.

The Coptic District

When the Arabs arrived in Egypt in the year 640, they conquered the Roman fortress called Babylon, which was built by Trajan at the beginning of the 2nd century. It occupied an area of 200 x 400 metres, with 11 metres high walls. Then, the Nile passed by the fortress and its main gate, known as the gate of Iron, faced the river. The Egyptian government is working today on a project to reconstruct the gate and open it to visitors. In the fortress enclosure, of which a few parts are still standing, multiple churches were built, in various cases, using walls and towers of the Roman fortress. The **Hanging church (Al-Muallaqa)** was built in the 7th century (although documents place the date after the 9th) on top of one of the towers at the main gate of the enclosure. Inside, very pretty icons are conserved. To the south of the basilica, there is a door

Al-Rifai Mosque: tomb of Reza Bahlawy, the last Shah of Persia. ■

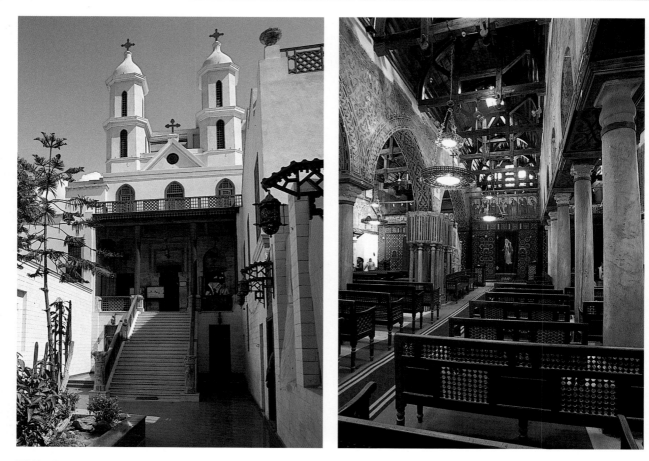

■ The Hanging Church (Al-Mualaqa).

The Hanging Church: interior. ■

that leads to another sanctuary, from which the gates of the ancient fortress can be distinguished.

Above another tower is the **church of Mari Girgis (Saint George)**, the Greek-Orthodox church that gave its name to the main street.

Going down a staircase of the street Mari Girgis, we reach the **church of St. Sergius (Abu Serga)**, from the 3rd or the 4th century, although documents only mention it after the 9th. This church is of great importance, since according to tradition, the Holy Family rested in it on their trip to Egypt. The sanctuary is divided from the central nave by a curtain of wood inlaid with ivory, built over the crypt where Jesus, Mary and Joseph rested.

Further along the same street stand **St. Barbara's Church** and the **Ben Ezra Synagogue**, which was built in 1892 in the place of the temple from the 11th century, are situated. During the reconstruction of the synagogue, 200,000 documents about the Jewish religion and laws were found, the majority of which are now kept at Cambridge University. The synagogue, like all of them, has two floors, the upper one for

■ Church of Mari Girgis (St George).

women and the lower one for men, where the sanctuary was also located.

The **Coptic Museum** was inaugurated in 1910 and the new part, in 1947. It exhibits pieces from convents and churches long gone, as well as others from private collections. The pieces are displayed according to their material: in rooms 1-9, stone pieces; in room 10, manuscripts; in rooms 11 and 12, cloth and fabric; in room 13, icons and marble pieces; and in rooms 14 to 16, metal pieces (jewels and weapons).

Coptic Museum: main entrance and room. ■

THE PYRAMIDS OF GIZA

The pyramids were the Pharaohs' tombs during the first half of the Pharaonic period. Among the 98 pyramids that have been discovered, the large ones at Giza stand out, as the ones with the biggest dimensions and the best conserved. The Giza platen is included within the great necropolis of Memphis, the first capital of Egypt and the place chosen by the Pharaohs of the 4th Dynasty.

The pyramid makes up one of the elements of a funeral complex designed to serve the Pharaoh in the other life. The so-called Temple of the Valley, where the Nile valley ends and the desert begins, was where the dead Pharaoh was purified and mummified. A ramp comes from this temple and connects with the other, called the mortuary temple, right in front of the pyramid, where the offerings were placed. In the pyramid itself, the Pharaoh was buried next to his funerary furniture.

The pyramid in ancient Egypt symbolized the rays of the sun leaving the solar disc and reaching the earth. Burying the Pharaoh underneath or inside assured his reunion with Ra, the sun god. And so, the Pharaoh would return to life, just as the sun rises again after it sets. For this reason, all of the pyramids were smooth and covered with the whitest and most polished stone and the upper part of some were covered with gold plating.

The **pyramid of Cheops**, the only one of the seven

■ Aerial view of the pyramids of Giza.

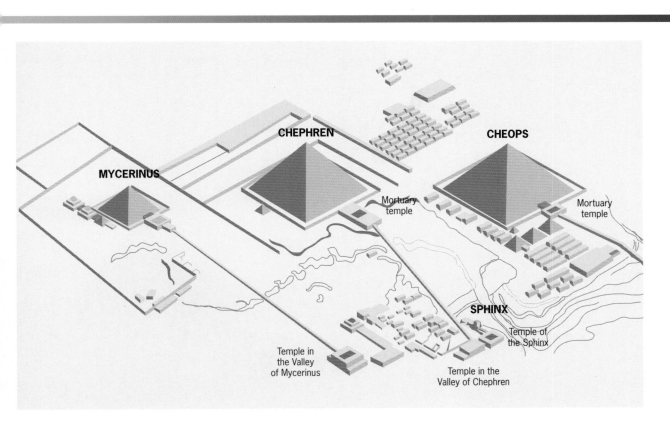

MYCERINUS

CHEPHREN

CHEOPS

Mortuary
temple

Mortuary
temple

SPHINX

Temple of
the Sphinx

Temple in
the Valley
of Mycerinus

Temple in the
Valley of Chephren

The pyramids of Giza. ■

The Pyramid of Cheops. ■

■ Sunset at the pyramids of Giza.

The pyramid of Cheops. ■

wonders of the world still in existence, is the biggest of all. According to Herodotus, it was built by 200,000 workers over 20 years, consisting of about 2,200,000 blocks of limestone, each one weighing two and a half tons. The pyramid reached 223 metres on each side (now 220 m) and 146 in height (now 137 m). On the north side, there are two entrances, a triangular one 17 metres high, which was the original, and the current one, a few metres lower, which was opened by the Arabs in the 8th century.

Inside, there are three chambers situated at different levels. The lowest one is not open to the public at present. At the end of the passageway leading from the entrance is the central chamber, and over this, preceded by a larger access ramp known as the great gallery, is the funeral chamber designed to house the sarcophagus of the Pharaoh. This chamber, covered with granite, displays two small openings to the outside, air inlets to allow the exit and entrance of the *ba* or vital breath of the Pharaoh.

Outside the pyramid of Cheops, five boats were buried.

On the south side, in 1954, the pieces of a large wooden boat, which when assembled, measured almost 43 metres in length. The wood used was Lebanon cedar. It has been conserved pretty well thanks to the dryness of the desert sand. It was one of the boats used for bringing the funerary furniture to the bank of the dead and so the Pharaoh could also use it as a means of transportation in the other world.

Outside almost all the pyramids, the tombs of relatives and nobles of the Pharaoh are found. In the case of Cheops, to the east, three pyramids of his wives and, behind them, various mastabas (tombs) of nobles from his reign, are situated. The most important is that of Meres-Ankh, wife of Chephren. Likewise, there are other mastabas on the west side. The **pyramid of Chephren** is somewhat smaller than that of Cheops, although it appears bigger because it was built on higher terrain. It is the only one that conserves part of the smooth surface near the point. Each one of its sides measures 200 metres and reaches a height of almost 140 metres. Its interior is also

The great gallery in the pyramid of Cheops.

The barque of Cheops.

Mastaba of Meres-Ankh: statues and scenes from everyday life. ■

much simpler. Going down a ramp, we reach an antechamber situated on the right. The hallway leads to the funeral chamber, where graffiti appears with the name of the Italian Belzoni, who discovered its interior in 1818.

The **pyramid of Mycerinus** is much smaller than the other two: 120 metres on each side and 66 metres high. On it, various blocks of rose-coloured granite surface, brought from Aswan, are conserved. Its interior displays two consecutive chambers, though his

sarcophagus sank off the Spanish coast with the boat that was transporting it to England. To the side, three smaller pyramids corresponding to the Queens of this Pharaoh are situated.

The **Temple of the Valley of Chephren**, situated next to the Great Sphinx, is conserved in fairly good condition, unlike the other two. It was built in limestone and covered with granite, and it has an alabaster floor. The temple takes the shape of a large "T". The five statues of Chephren, which were found here by

Pyramid of Chephren. ■

Illumination of the pyramid of Chephren at night.

Mariette, the founder of the Egyptian Museum, are exhibited in this museum, and it is customary for tourists to throw coins to them to express the wish to return to Egypt.

The **Sphinx** is a sculpture of considerable size (57 metres long and 24 metres high), found on the rock where it was carved so as not to obstruct the views of the pyramid of Chephren. Its name comes from *Shespanj*, which means, "living figure". It has a lion's body and a human's head, which symbolize the strength

Pyramid of Mycerinus and smaller pyramids of the queens.

The Sphinx. ■

and the wisdom of the Pharaoh. Considered at first to be the guardian of the area, it was later deified as a form of the Sun God.

On the southern route towards Memphis, there is another part of the great necropolis, called **Abu Sir**, which was the preferred place of the Pharaohs of the 5th Dynasty to build their pyramids, as well as a temple dedicated to the god Ra. In this area are three fairly well conserved pyramids, much smaller than those of Giza.

Pyramid and remains of the funerary temple of Sahu-Ra in Abu Sir. ■

MEMPHIS AND SAQQARA

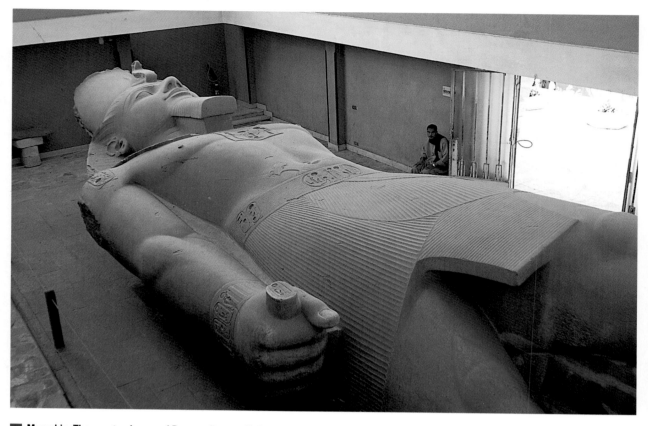

■ Memphis. The great colossus of Ramses II: overall view and partial view of the face.

Memphis, Greek word that comes from the Egyptian *Men-nefer*, which means "stable" and "pretty", was the capital of Egypt in the Old Kingdom and it continued to be an important city throughout the Pharaonic era. The Pharaohs of the New Kingdom made an effort to increase its splendour, especially Ramses II. Later, it was one of the largest and most beautiful cities in the East, even though it began to lose importance to Alexandria under the rule of the Ptolemies. Successive wars, invasions and floods of the Nile devastated and finally erased the city from the face of the earth. Today, only a few ruins remain of what was a magnificent city and in its place is a beautiful palm tree forest.

At the end of this palm tree forest, before parking, to the left, are the remains of the temple for mummifying the bull Apis, the sacred animal of the god Ptah, the main deity of Memphis and, according to his priests, the creator of the world.

In the place of the main temple, an open-air museum keeps beautiful sculptures, among which the **grand colossus of Ramses II**, of about 12 metres, stands out, currently lying on the ground protected by a pavilion, erected for this motive. The details and proportions of this statue are superb. The **alabaster sphinx** is another important piece in Memphis. Carved at the command of one of the

Memphis. The alabaster Sphinx.

Pharaohs of the 18th dynasty, it weighs about 80 tons. We can also admire statues of Ramses II, III and VI, as well as sarcophagi and stone blocks that all bear the names or representations of the god Ptah, his wife, the goddess Sekhmet (of war) and his son, the god Nefertem (of the lotus flower).

Leaving Memphis towards the west, right where the great palm tree forest ends and the desert begins, stretches the greater part of the necropolis of Memphis: **Saqqara.** Its name comes from the god Soker, one of the cemetery gods. The landscape is very impressive: on one side, we see numerous palm trees, while on the other, the contrasting aridness of the desert, the ideal place in ancient Egypt for building tombs.

Arriving, we can already distinguish the **step pyramid,** the most characteristic element of Saqqara, which includes the funeral complex of Djoser, the first Pharaoh of the 3rd Dynasty. It was built by Imhotep, his architect, who used stone for the first time in an Egyptian construction. The complex has an enclosure wall of 554 x 277 metres and about 10 metres in height. It has recessed panelling as decorations in the entire wall, 13 false doors and only one entrance, just like the palace where the Pharaoh lived. After the entrance, a colonnade begins, with columns in the form of papyrus stalks tied together, forming some 42 chapels for statues of deities, ending in an open courtyard.

On the other side of the patio rises the pyramid. In the beginning, it was built as a mastaba, and later, five more were added to arrive at about 66 metres in height and a rectangular base of 121 x 109 metres. To the north of the pyramid are situated the ruins of the mortuary temple, where offerings were made, and a chamber with two holes through which we see a replica of the statue of Djoser, whose original is exhibited in the Egyptian Museum of Cairo.

Beyond the complex of Djoser, there are more monuments: the **pyramid of Unas**, the **mastaba of Idut** (his daughter) and other mastabas on both sides of the elevated path that connects the Mortuary Temple of Unas with his temple of the valley, of which a part is conserved.

The **mastaba of Ti** is one of the prettiest in Saqqara. It belongs to a priest from the 5th dynasty. Like all mastabas, it shows scenes of daily life in Ancient Egypt, but this one conserves very interesting polychrome and the details are very well depicted. Also, it is the only mastaba whose subterranean chamber is open to the public. This is where the sarcophagus is kept. The **mastabas of Ptah-Hotep and Mereruka** are well worth a visit, the first because it possesses the

■ Saqqara. Main entrance to the complex, and the Step Pyramid.

best-conserved chapel in all Saqqara, decorated in very lively colours, and the second for its dimensions (32 chapels) and interior chambers. In their decoration, both display many aspects of daily life such as agriculture, hunting animals and birds, fishing, jewellery, etc. The bearers of offerings are also depicted. The **pyramid of Teti**, of the 6th dynasty, together with that of Unas, present interior walls covered with hieroglyphics known as *the texts of the pyramids*. These are hymns that the priests normally sang after the death of a Pharaoh. But these two Pharaohs and Pepi I also wished to have them inside the pyramid with

■ Saqqara. Courtyard of Heb-sed and the Step Pyramid.

Saqqara. Reliefs on the so-called Tomb of the Butchers. ■

Saqqara. Mastaba of Ptah-Hotep: geese placed in cages ready ■ for transport.

them. The texts tell about the journey to the other world, which the Pharaoh would have to make in order to finally arrive at his eternal happiness.

The **Serapeum**, the place where the sacred bulls of the god Ptah were buried, known as Apis, although it is closed now, is one of the most interesting places in Saqqara. It has some hallways with monumental sarcophagi on each side, in many of which were found mummified bulls, kept today in the Agricultural Museum.

Great sarcophagus of a sacred bull mummified in the Serapeum ■ at Saqqara.

■ Saqqara. Mastaba of Ti: cattle crossing a river and servants taking offerings to their lord.

DAHSHUR

■ Dahshur. The Bent Pyramid.

Dahshur lies just a few kilometres south of Saqqara. This forms another part of the cemetery of Memphis, where Sneferu, the father of Cheops (27th century BC) ordered the first perfect pyramid in the area raised. During its construction, the architects warned that the pyramid was being elevated at an extremely large angle (54°) and because of the appearance of some cracks and they reduced the angle to 43°. And thus the so-called **bent pyramid** came into being.

Next to the bent pyramid, Sneferu ordered the construction of the first real pyramid, known as the **red pyramid** as it was covered with local reddish stone blocks. Each side measures 220 metres and the whole reaches a height of 99 metres. Its interior, formed by three chambers one after another, is particularly spectacular.

The Pharaohs Sesostris II, Amenemhat II and Amenemhat III of the Middle Kingdom also chose this place to build their pyramids. These, however, were made using another technique, adobe, and covered with stone. But with time, the stone collapsed, leaving the pyramids as large heaps of earth. In the surroundings, inside the tombs of the princesses, many jewels were discovered that today are exhibited in the Metropolitan Museum and the Egyptian Museum of Cairo.

■ Dahshur. The Red Pyramid.

In **Meidum**, nearly 90 km south Cairo, we find the pyramid known to the Egyptians as the **False Pyramid** due to its unusual shape. This step pyramid, 90 metres high, was built by Huni, the last Pharaoh in the 3rd Dynasty, and completed by Snefru (17th century BC). The entrance to it is in the north side, whilst the oldest and simplest mortuary temple, in the form of two stelae with an altar between, is on the east side.

Beside the pyramid are the remains of several mastabas. One of these contained the famous statues of Rahotep and Nofret, whilst another was adorned with a frieze of the so-called "Geese of Meidum", now in the Egyptian Museum of Cairo.

The pyramid at Meidum. ■

Beni Hassan. Paintings illustrating scenes from everyday ■
life.

Beni Hassan is a necropolis some 300 km south of Cairo, where the nobles of region were buried during the Middle Kingdom. There are a total of 39 tombs cut into the rock, of which only 12 are decorated, not with the reliefs found in most tombs, but with paintings. Like the decoration in Old Kingdom tombs, these murals depict different aspects of every day life æfarming, arts and crafts, etcæ along with a new theme: military and feudal life, scenes from which can be seen in the tombs of Amenemhet "Amini", Khnumhotep I, Bakit and Khnumhptep III.

Beni Hassan. Paintings illustrating different sports. ■

EL-BERSHA / EL-ASHMUNEIN

■ One of the statues of monkeys that flanked the entrance to the old Temple of Hermopolis.

In **El-Bersha**, just a few kilometres south of Beni Hassan, we find another twelve tombs. The most important is the tomb of Djehutihotep, governor of the province during the rein of three Pharaohs of the 12th Dynasty. This tomb is adorned with the famous scene of the transportation of colossus on sledges, pulled over rollers made from tree trunks.

El-Ashmunein was an important city in Ancient Egypt as, like Heliopolis and Memphis, provided its own version of the creation of the world, and it was also the centre of the cult of Thoth, god of wisdom and writing. Represented in monkey form or with the head of an ibis, Thoth was later identified with Hermes by the Greeks, who named this city Hermopolis. We can form little idea of what the Temple of Thoth must have been like, as little remains of it except the two statues of monkeys that stood before the temple and now bear the name of Amenophis III.

In the 3rd century BC, Ptolemy III ordered a temple built over the remains of another, built by Ramses II. In the 5th century AD, this temple was converted into a church with Latin cross basilical ground plan.

■ Remains of the basilica of Hermopolis.

Reliefs on the tomb of Petosiris. ■

Tuna El-Gebel is the cemetery of Hermopolis. The first thing the visitor see just before arriving is one of Akhenaten's boundary stelae, which marked the limits of this Pharaoh's city (now Tell El-Amarna). The most important monument here is the tomb of Petosiris. The tomb of a priest and his family, this tomb dates back to the late-4th century BC.

■ Catacombs of Thoth.

It consists of a pronaos or anti-chamber with capitals and scenes from everyday life, and a naos with vertical shaft connecting to the funeral chamber, adorned with scenes nearly all funereal. Also in Tuna El-Gebel is the tomb of Isadora, with a mummy dating to the 2nd century AD, and the burial place of the god Thoth's mummified ibises and monkeys.

TELL EL-AMARNA

Amenophis IV dealt a devastating blow to the powerful priests of Amun-Ra, whose wealth and influence had been constantly increased by previous Pharaohs, when he began to worship a single god, Aten, the sun disc, changing his name to Akhenaten and building a temple to adore the god in Thebes. Aten is represented by a solar disc from which shine rays, each terminating with a human hand bringing the Ankh (life sign) to the Pharaoh's nose. After a four-year struggle against the mighty priests of Amun-Ra, Akhenaten left Thebes, founding a new city some 300 kilometres to the north, naming it Akhetaten (the horizon of Aten). Now known as **Tell El-Amarna**, Akhetaten was the Egyptian capital for 20 years, up to the death of the Pharaoh.

These 20 years of life and development were sufficient to establish a fully-fledged city. The main temple, of which only a few ruins remain, was 800 x 275 metres in size. Opposite, joined to it by a bridge, was the main royal palace. The villas of Akhenaten's friends and followers were large, whilst the houses of the workers and craftsmen were much simpler. Much of

■ Ruins of the small Temple of Tell El-Amarna.

this city, abandoned for centuries, now lies in ruins, however.

The royal tomb lies at some distance from this site, in a well-chosen location. There are two hills here, and when the sun rises, it passes between the two, resembling the hieroglyphic for the horizon. One of Akhenaten's daughters is buried here, the tomb conserving reliefs, though greatly deteriorated. Excavation work has yet to discover whether Akhenaten himself is buried in this area.

The tombs are distributed in three zones, the most important and easy to visit being those in the northern group, such as those of Huya, Ahmose and Penehesy. The prettiest, however, is the tomb of Meryre, priest of the solar disc and royal scribe. Two of the four pillars that supported the ceiling survive, as well as several scenes, including representations of the Temple of Aten and another showing the arrival of the Pharaoh followed by his wife, Nefertiti, and an image presided over by the god Aten.

The south tomb group is also interesting, particularly that of Ay, "God's father", who governed Egypt after Tutankhamun.

■ Tell El-Amarna. Tomb of Meryre.

Tomb of Meryre: relief showing Akhenaten in his chariot, followed by Nefertiti in hers, under the god Aten.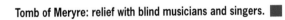

Tomb of Meryre: relief with blind musicians and singers. ■

ABYDOS

Temple of Seti I.

Temple of Seti I: hypostyle hall.

Abydos lies some 140 km north of Luxor, on the west bank of the Nile. According to the myth of Isis and Osiris, this was where the latter's head was found after his body had been cut into 14 pieces, and Abydos consequently became a centre of the cult of Osiris as the god of the Netherworld and a place of pilgrimage for people from all over Ancient Egypt. Those unable to afford to make the journey themselves would send funerary stelae to be buried beside the god Osiris. Moreover, its location close to Thinis, the first capital of united Egypt, Abydos is where the first Pharaohs were buried.

The **Temple of Seti I** is the largest conserved in Abydos today. This 19th Dynasty (1290-1279 BC) Pharaoh began its construction, which was completed by his son, Ramses II. Like all mortuary temples, the Temple of Seti I consists of a pylon gateway, a courtyard, another pylon, another courtyard, two hypostyle halls (one built under Ramses, the other under Seti) and, at the end, seven chapels. These are devoted, from right to left, to Horus, Isis, Osiris (the Abydos triad), Amun, Ra, Ptah and Seti I himself. The reliefs here are considered amongst the most beautiful in all Egypt, due to the fine drawing style evinced, the details and the good colour conservation. Two more chapels in the south

Temple of Seti I: relief of the "Abydos Kinglist". ■

■ Temple of Seti I: examples of the reliefs that adorn the temple walls, considered the most beautiful in Egypt due to their fine detail and well conserved colours.

wing are devoted to Sokaris and Nefertem. Most outstanding of all, however, is the so-called "Abydos Kinglist" in the second hypostyle hall, which portrays Seti I and Ramses II before more than 70 cartouches corresponding to all the previous Pharaohs. The list begins with Narmer and ends with Seti I, though some are missed out, including Hatshepsut, Akhenaten and Tutankhamun.

Temple of Ramses II.

The Temple of Seti I leads to the cenotaph or symbolic tomb of Osiris, known as the **Osireion**. This consists of an entrance, a hall adorned with scenes from the *Book of Gates*, and the main hall, containing the sarcophagus on an "island" surrounded by water, with no bridge across. Seti I's son also had a mortuary temple built. The **Temple of Ramses II**, located to the northwest of his father's temple, is smaller and adorned with scenes from the wars this Pharaoh fought, particularly against the Hittites.

Scene in the Temple of Ramses II.

DENDERA

■ Temple of Hathor.

■ Mammisi of Augustus.

Dendera lies some 60 km north of Luxor. Of the old city, Tentyris, all that remains are adobe ruins inside the walls, stretches of which are conserved as high as 10 metres.

The Temple of Dendera is the best-conserved in the city. It was built in the First Century BC and dedicated to the goddess Hathor, god of love and motherhood, as well as of joy and music, for which reason her symbol was the sistrum. On the right before we

reach the temple is the Roman **mammisi**, or birth house, built in Graeco-Roman times. A mammisi is a chapel to celebrate the birth of the son of the god or goddess to whom the temple is dedicated. Further ahead are the ruins of an earlier mammisi and, between the two, a Christian church.

The **Temple of Dendera or of Hathor** follows the model employed during the Graeco-Roman period: a pylon (now lost), a courtyard and two hypostyle halls. The first of these has 24 columns with Hathoric capitals, representing the goddess with the head and ears of a cow and the face of a woman. The ceiling is decorated with cosmic and astrological themes, such as the twelve signs of the zodiac and the goddess Nut giving birth to the sun in the morning and devouring it again at dusk. The second hypostyle hall has just six columns, all very low, with capitals featuring floral motifs. Next we come to the pronaos, whilst the sanctuary is at the end of the temple. The sanctuary is surrounded by several chambers used to store objects used in the cult. The crypt open to visitors (of a total of twelve) is where the most valuable objects were kept. Though very narrow, it is decorated with extraordinary reliefs.

There are two staircases in the temple, one used to carry the statue of the goddess to the temple roof to

Temple of Hathor: hypostyle hall. ■

meet the rays of the sun in a ceremony in which Hathor was replenished with positive energy after a year enclosed in the darkness of the sanctuary. The statue was then taken down again using the second staircase.

Above are two chambers dedicated to "The Resurrection of Osiris". The ceiling of the first was originally decorated by the famous zodiac, now in the Louvre Museum. What we see here today is a copy.

On the rear wall of the temple is the only relief in Egypt depicting Cleopatra VII. The queen is portrayed with her son, Caesarion, making an offering to the goddess Hathor and other deities.

The temple's sacred lake, known as Cleopatra's Pool, is also conserved, surrounded by palm trees that embellish the site even further.

■ Temple of Hathor: reliefs in the crypt.

Temple of Hathor: relief of a goddess on one of the external ■
walls.

LUXOR

■ Feluccas on the Nile at Luxor.

The celebrated city of **Luxor**, known as Thebes to the Greeks and as Waset during the times of the Pharaohs, lies 670 km south of Cairo and has a population of 80,000. On arriving here, the Arabs named the city El-Uksur, "palaces", and which later became Luxor, perhaps thinking that the temples of Karnak and Luxor were palaces of the Pharaohs. The capital of Upper Egypt's fourth province was capital of the whole country at the beginning of the Middle Kingdom, flourishing particularly from the 20th century BC, but gained its maximum importance when the Thebans freed Egypt from the Hyksos, making Luxor the capital, which it remained throughout most of the New Kingdom period. As this was a time when each successive Pharaoh sought to out-

■ Calash.

do his predecessors in works, Luxor became one of the most monumental cities in the ancient world. Luxor was also the sacred city of Amun-Ra. Amun was a local god elevated to the status of national deity by the Pharaohs, who increased his importance and antiquity by combining him with Ra. With his wife, Mut, goddess of motherhood and his son, Khonsu, the moon god, Amun-Ra formed the Thebes triad. Amun was also worshipped in combination with Min, god of fertility, who was then known as Amun-Min. As was customary in Ancient Egypt, the population of Luxor lived on the east bank, whilst the west bank was reserved for funeral cults and as a burial place, and so things continued for fifteen centuries. Particularly interesting on the east bank are the temples of Karnak and Luxor and the Luxor Museum, whilst on the west bank is the whole necropolis of Thebes, that is to say, the Valley of the Kings, the Valley of the Queens, the Valley of the Nobles and the Valley of the Craftsmen, as well as the mortuary temples the Pharaohs built in this area. We should remember that, during the New Kingdom period, the Pharaohs no longer built their mortuary temples beside their tombs as was the practice amongst their predecessors, rather they built them further away. The temples were used to carry out the rites for the dead Pharaoh, and were visited during the Festival of the Valley, when the statue of Amun-Ra was taken across the Nile as part of a ceremony that took place in them until the Ptolemaic period.

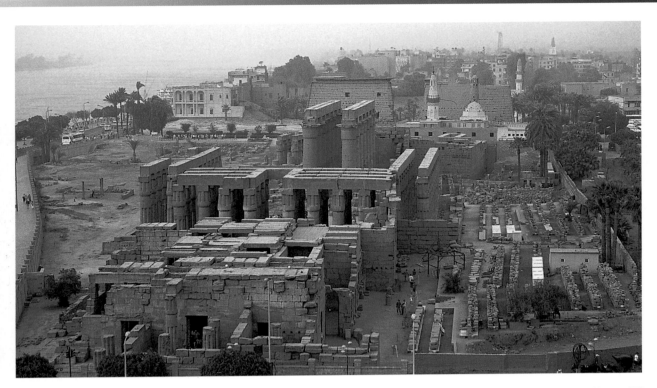

Overall view of the Temple of Luxor. ■

Karnak

With an area of 65 hectares, this is the largest man-made site in the world. Under Ramses III, 159 villages and 420,000 head of animals belonged to the temple. The precinct contains temples dedicated to Mut, Khonsu and Montu, but the most important is the Temple of Amun-Ra, built on the remains of an earlier 12th-Dynasty temple site. Construction began under Thutmose I and was continued by several Pharaohs until it reached its present size. Returning victorious

Temple of Karnak: main entrance. ■

■ Karnak: courtyard of the small Temple of Ramses III.

■ Temple of Karnak: relief representing the god Amun.

from war, the Pharaohs would show Amun-Ra their gratitude by extending the temple with new buildings. The Temple of Amun-Ra is organised along two axes, the main one running from west to east. The entrance to the site is from a small landing quay on a canal that communicates with the Nile. From here, an avenue flanked by two lines of sphinxes with the heads of rams, the animal that symbolised Amun, leads to the first pylon or entrance. This pylon is unfinished, and it is even possible to see the remains of the original adobe brick ramp built to raise the blocks to build it. In the first courtyard, on the left, are the chapels of Seti II, built to house the sacred barques of the Thebes Triad: that of Mut on the left, that of Amun in the centre and that of Khonsu on the right. On the other side of the courtyard stands a small temple built by Ramses III and decorated by several statues and festive scenes. In the centre of the courtyard stand the remains of the columns from a pavilion built by Taharqa (25th Dynasty) and a huge block of alabaster. Behind is a colossal statue of Ramses II Behind is a colossal statue of Ramses II with one of his daughters.

We next cross a second pylon, the stones from which were taken from what was once part of a temple and several chapels. These have now been reconstructed on the site known as the Open-Air Museum. This second pylon provides access to a stone forest, the largest hypostyle hall in Egypt, with a total of 134 columns, the 12 in the centre the tallest, standing at a height of 22 metres, whilst the others are 18 metres high. These twelve higher columns have open papyri-

Open Air Museum at Karnak: reliefs in the White Chapel. ■

form capitals, whilst the others have closed papyri-form capitals. The different in height between them enabled windows to be opened to let light and air into this hall, which is completely covered by stone blocks. The hall was built by Seti I and his son Ramses II, whose enormous cartouches are seen above near-ly all the columns. The outer walls are decorated by representations of the wars both Pharaohs fought,

■ Open Air Museum at Karnak: the Red Chapel.

■ Temple of Karnak: hypostyle hall.

Temple of Karnak: obelisks of Tuthmosis or Thutmose I and Hatshepsut.

those of Seti I on the north wall and those of Ramses II on the south.

Passing through the third pylon, built by Amenophis III, we come to the part built by Thutmosis I and Hatshepsut. Here we find the remains of pylons and the obelisks of Thutmosis I (22 metres) and Hatshepsut (29 metres, the highest in Egypt). Their cartouches and titles are inscribed on several columns, up-down. The rest of the temple was built by Thutmosis III, though the sanctuary was later altered by Philip III Arrhidaeus, Alexander the Great's brother and successor. Along this same east-west axis, leaving behind the space once occupied by a 12th-Dynastic temple, we come to the Festival Temple of Thutmosis III. The temple was decorated with very interesting reliefs, particularly a kinglist beginning with Narmer and including all successive Pharaohs with the exception of Hatshepsut. This list is now kept in the Louvre Museum, however.

The other axis in the Temple of Karnak, from north to south, consists of four pylons and three courtyards, in the first of which 779 statues and thousands of bronze statuettes were found in 1903.

The sacred lake, watered by the River Nile, lies to the east of this north-south axis. The waters were used to purify the statues of the gods and the priests themselves. Beside the lake is a giant scarab beetle, carved in granite, from the Mortuary Temple of Amenophis III on the other side of the Nile.

■ The sacred lake of Karnak.

Luxor. Avenue of the Sphinxes. ■

Temple of Luxor

Another sacred site, known in ancient times as Ipet-resyt, meaning "southern chapel" and dedicated to Amun in his two forms was built three kilometres south of Karnak to celebrate the most important festivity in Thebes, known as the Opet. During this feast, the statues of the triad were taken from the Temple of Karnak and transported down the Nile to the Temple of Luxor. As they were taken down the Nile on the sacred barque, the people danced and sang with joy on the bank. The statues remained in the Temple of Luxor for some 20 days before returning to that of Karnak along the three-kilometre path connecting the two, once flanked by sphinxes along its entire length and known as the Avenue of Sphinxes. The Temple of Luxor was built during the reign of Amenophis III, though additions were later made to

Temple of Luxor: pylon and obelisk of Ramses II. ■

Temple of Luxor: the main entrance at night.

Courtyard of Ramses II: papyriform capital behind a statue of the Pharaoh.

the site, most of them by Ramses II. A church was built beside the sanctuary antechamber in the 6th century, whilst in the 15th century the Abu El-Haggag mosque, still used as such, was built in the courtyard of Ramses II. Ever since the construction of the first temple here in the 14th century BC, then, this site has continued to be a holy place.

Facing the main entrance to the temple stands a 25-metre high obelisk built by Ramses II. This formed a pair with a second obelisk that Mohammed Ali, King of Egypt, gave to Louis-Philippe of France in 1831 and now stands in Place de la Concorde square in Paris. Of the six colossi that once stood here, more-

over, only three remain. One represents a standing Ramses II, the other two the same Pharaoh sitting on the throne with Nefertari beside one of his legs. The pylon we come to next, one of the most harmonious, is decorated with scenes from Ramses II's famous battle against the Hittites at Kadesh. The pylon gives entry to the Courtyard of Ramses II. On the right are the chapels built by Queen Hatshepsut before the temple itself, in order to house the sacred barques of the gods. The courtyard features two rows of columns with closed papyriform capitals between which were statues of the Pharaoh, only a few of which survive. The Courtyard of Ramses II terminates with two black granite colossi representing the Pharaoh sitting on his throne, crushing Egypt's enemies with his feet.

Passing through the Courtyard of Ramses II, we come to the Courtyard of 14 Columns, built by Amenophis III. These columns are 23 metres high and are adorned with open papyriform capitals. The courtyard contains works by Tutankhamun and Horemheb. The Courtyard of Amenophis III is truly impressive, with two rows of columns with closed papyriform capitals. The statues that once stood here can now be seen in the Luxor Museum, after being discovered underground in 1989.

The Courtyard of Amenophis III is followed by a hypostyle hall with 32 columns identical to those in the previous court. It leads into the former Christian

Courtyard of Amenophis III. ■

church, which closes the rest of the temple. Its walls were decorated with Christian frescoes in the 6th century. The antechamber leading to sanctuary is adorned by scenes of offerings and remains of polychrome work. The sanctuary built by Amenophis III was later replaced by Alexander the Great, who is represented on the walls before Amun in his two forms. The rear of the temple is taken up by rooms used to store the objects needed for ritual ceremonies.

Luxor Museum

This recently-built museum houses many artworks found in the city. The most important piece is the statue of Thutmosis III, his features finely carved in basalt. Another important work is the statue of Amenophis III with the god Sobek (the crocodile), in alabaster. The Cachet room features works found in the Temple of Luxor, including those of Horemheb kneeling before Amun-Ra and the quartz statue of Amenophis III. Here, too, is the mummy of Ramses I, which Egypt recovered recently from the United States.

Museum of Luxor: Tuthmosis III and Amenophis III with ■
the god Sobek.

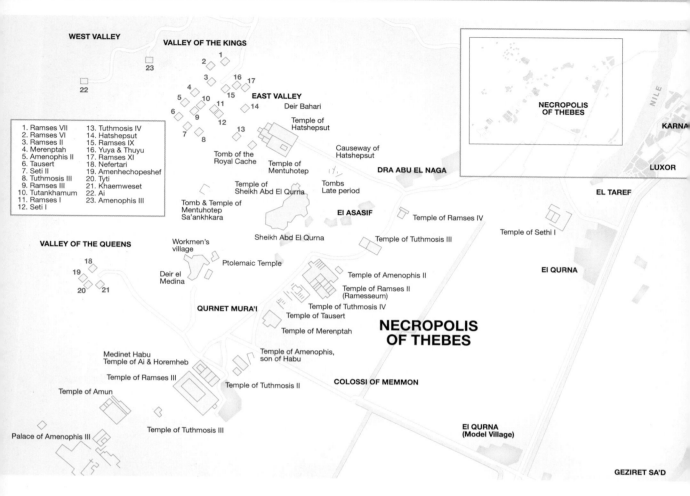

Map legend (Valley of the Kings / Valley of the Queens):

1. Ramses VII
2. Ramses VI
3. Ramses II
4. Merenptah
5. Amenophis II
6. Tausert
7. Seti II
8. Tuthmosis III
9. Ramses III
10. Tutankhamum
11. Ramses I
12. Seti I
13. Tuthmosis IV
14. Hatshepsut
15. Ramses IX
16. Yuya & Thuyu
17. Ramses XI
18. Nefertari
19. Amenhechopeshef
20. Tyti
21. Khaemweset
22. Ai
23. Amenophis III

Map labels: WEST VALLEY · VALLEY OF THE KINGS · EAST VALLEY · Deir Bahari · Temple of Hatshepsut · Causeway of Hatshepsut · Tomb of the Royal Cache · Temple of Mentuhotep · DRA ABU EL NAGA · Temple of Sheikh Abd El Qurna · Tombs Late period · Tomb & Temple of Mentuhotep Sa'ankhkara · EL ASASIF · Sheikh Abd El Qurna · Temple of Ramses IV · Temple of Tuthmosis III · Temple of Sethi I · EL TAREF · VALLEY OF THE QUEENS · Workmen's village · Ptolemaic Temple · Deir el Medina · Temple of Amenophis II · Temple of Ramses II (Ramesseum) · Temple of Tuthmosis IV · Temple of Tausert · QURNET MURA'I · Temple of Merenptah · EL QURNA · NECROPOLIS OF THEBES · Temple of Amenophis, son of Habu · Medinet Habu Temple of Ai & Horemheb · Temple of Ramses III · COLOSSI OF MEMMON · Temple of Amun · Temple of Tuthmosis II · Temple of Tuthmosis III · Palace of Amenophis III · EL QURNA (Model Village) · GEZIRET SA'D · NECROPOLIS OF THEBES · KARNA · LUXOR · NILE

Valley of the Kings

Alarmed by the fact that the pyramids where the previous Pharaohs were buried had all been raided, the New Kingdom Pharaohs stopped building them, instead having their tombs made on a distant site on the west bank known as Valley of the Kings. To date, 62 tombs have been unearthed here, all excavated into the limestone rock of the valley. These rock tombs are made up of corridors with side chambers ending in the burial chamber, which may be supported by columns if its size so requires. This is where the great sarcophagus for the royal mummy is kept. The walls are covered by a layer of plaster enabling polychrome scenes to be drawn on them, narrating the Pharaoh's desire to accompany the god Ra on his journey to the Netherworld from sunset to dawn, when they will both emerge once more. This explains the different forms Ra takes: scarab beetle (in the morning); falcon with solar disc on its head (at midday); and ram's head and staff (in the afternoon).

The first tombs were more simply decorated. It is thought that the walls of these tombs were covered in papyrus, with drawings and texts from the *Book of the Netherworld* in black and red only, as is the case of the tombs of **Thutmose III** and **Amenophis II**. The columns in these two tombs feature representations of the Pharaoh with gods from the Netherworld, such as Osiris and Anubis. Later tombs are adorned by more sophisticated scenes. These include those of **Horemheb**, **Ramses I** and, particularly, **Seti I**, the biggest and best-conserved in the valley. The walls of the corri-

Tomb of Horemheb: scene of the Pharaoh offering wine to Anubis.

Tomb of Ramses I: barque of the sun god, fragment from the "Book of Doors".

dors and chambers in this tomb are decorated with scenes and texts from different books of the dead, though some scenes are incomplete. The walls and doors of several corridors and chambers in this tomb are decorated by different parts of the books of the dead, though some scenes are unfinished. The tombs of the later Pharaohs, all named Ramses, are very similar to the earlier ones, with long, straight corridors, as we can seen in the tombs of **Ramses III**, **Ramses**

Scenes adorning the tomb of Seti I.

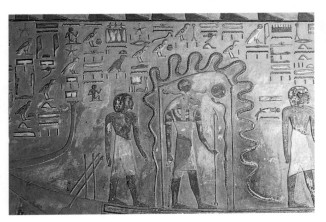

■ Scenes decorating the tomb of Ramses VI.

IV, **Ramses VII** and **Ramses IX**. That of **Ramses VI** is particularly outstanding. Very long, it is the only tomb in the Valley of the Kings in which the funeral books are represented completely, both on walls and ceilings. This tomb also boasts the most beautiful and best-conserved burial chamber in the whole valley.

The tomb of **Tutankhamun** was the last to be discovered, by Howard Carter in 1922. We can well understand Carter's joy when he brought out all the treasures and funeral gifts from the tomb to be taken to the Egyptian Museum of Cairo, as is the only royal tomb to have been found completely intact. In comparison with the rest of the valley, this is a fairly small tomb. It has an antechamber and funeral chamber with two side chambers. Three of the four walls in the funeral chamber are decorated with scenes. This is where Tutankhamun was buried, in the interior of four gilded wooden shrines, one inside the other, in a stone sarcophagus containing three gilded wooden coffins, one inside the other.

■ Carter when the doors to the golden chapels of Tutankhamun were opened.

Chariots and other objects in the ante-chamber to the tomb ■ of Tutankhamun, just as when it was discovered in 1922.

Tomb of Tutankhamun: funeral chamber. ■

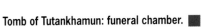

Overall aerial view of the Valley of the Queens.

Valley of the Queens

Several queens and their children, from the 19th Dynasty on, were buried here. To date, some 80 tombs have been identified, though most are still in the process of being studied. The most important, and the most beautiful, is the tomb of **Nefertari**, favourite wife of Ramses II. Its ground plan, more complex than usual, shares similarities with the tombs of the kings. The reliefs in

Tomb of Nefertari: the Queen playing Senet. ■

Tomb of Nefertari: representation of the Queen.

it show the queen in the company of various deities, as well as different parts of the *Book of the Dead*.

The tombs of **Amonherkhepeshef** and **Khamuas**, children of Ramses III, are good examples of the tombs of princes and princesses. Both feature scenes showing their father the Pharaoh presenting his children (whose hair is always seen as a side-lock, a symbol of childhood) to the different deities. The bright colours in these scenes have been very well conserved.

Tomb the noble Nakht: three women taking part in a typical Theban festivity.

Tomb of the noble Menna: threshing scene.

Tomb of Nefertari: Isis leads Queen Nefertari by the hand.

Valleys of the Nobles

The tombs of the nobles are the most important, both in size and variety of themes, after those of the kings. Most are stone-cut tombs with antechamber and chapel in the form of an inverted "T". The first part is covered, in the main, with biographical scenes about the deceased, whilst a second part shows scenes of funeral rituals and at the end of the tomb is a niche containing a statue of him and, on occasion, his wife.

Two zones contain noble tombs are **El-Asasif** and **El-Khokha**, but the most important is **el Qurna**, which contains the tombs of several high ranking

officials from the 18th Dynasty, such as those of **Nakht** and **Menna**. The latter was a scribe at the service of Amun and a royal scribe during the reign of Thutmose IV. His tomb is well-known for its interesting scenes of farming work, offerings, hunting and fishing.

One of the most important and best-conserved tombs is that of **Rekhmire**, Egyptian vizier under Thutmosis III. In the antechamber are scenes showing the trib-

Tomb of the Vizier Rekhmire: the tribes of Africa arriving at the court of the Pharaoh.

■ Tomb of the noble Sennefer: partial view of the vines decorating the ceiling.

Tomb of the noble Ramose: partial view of a relief. ■

utes offered by foreign peoples, whilst the chapel conserves the most complete scenes of funeral rites. The tomb of **Sennefer**, mayor of Thebes during the reign of Amenophis II, is known as the tomb of vines as this plant is represented on the ceiling. The tomb of **Ramose**, vizier and governor of Thebes under Amenophis IV, though unfinished due to the transfer of both Ramose and the Pharaoh to Tell El-Amarna, is very interesting, as its reliefs are finely executed, and because of a fresco representing a funeral procession, including the famous scene of the grieving mourners.

■ Tomb of the noble Ramose: part of the funeral procession.

Deir El-Medina or Valley of the Craftsmen. ■

Deir El-Medina or Valley of the Craftsmen

The only people who lived on the west bank were the architects, workers and artists that worked on the tombs and mortuary temples. They lived in a small township of which all that remains today are the ruins of the **houses**, grouped on either side of the main road. These were simple, adobe houses, with four rooms generally: living room, sitting room, bedroom with adjoining bathroom and, at the end, the kitchen with the oven.

The tombs of the craftsmen are those whose polychrome has been best conserved in all Egypt. Those of **Senejem** (reign of Ramses II), **Pashed** and

■ Adobe brick pyramid crowning a tomb in Deir El-Medina.

Tomb of Senejem: Osiris, the god of death. ■

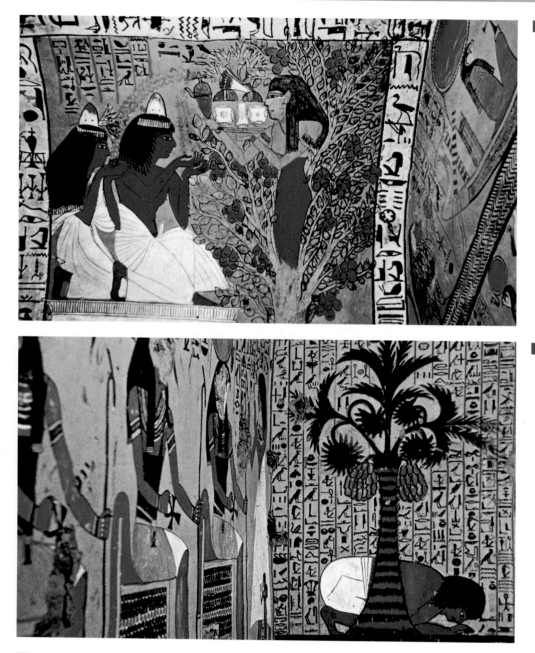

■ Tomb of Senejem: the goddess Nut appears before the dead couple to give them water on their arrival in the underworld.

■ Tomb of Pashed: the deceased drinks water from the tank below a palm tree.

Aerial view of the temples of Hatshepsut and Mentuhotep in Deir El-Bahari. ■

■ Tomb of Inherka: two scenes from the Book of the Dead.

 Temple of Hatshepsut.

Inherka are the best examples of this. All contain painted (not relief) funeral scenes including parts of the *Book of the Dead*.

The **Temple of Deir El-Medina**, dedicated to Hathor and Maat, was built in Ptolemaic times over older ruins. It contains interesting reliefs, particularly in the two chambers on either side of the sanctuary.

Deir El-Bahari

Deir El-Bahari is the site of the **Mortuary Temple of Queen Hatshepsut**, designed by her architect, Senmut, and dedicated to Amun-Ra. The entrance is formed by a pylon and an avenue of sphinxes, now lost. The temple consists of three terraces, each on a different level, before which stand square columned porticoes. The walls of the first terrace were adorned with scenes depicting the transportation along the River Nile of the obelisks the queen ordered installed in Karnak. In the second, on the right, are scenes depicting the queen's divine birth in which she is seen to be the daughter of Amun-Ra himself. On the left is a description of the trade expedition the queen sent to Punt (Somalia) to import myrrh trees to Egypt for the first time (remains of two myrrh trees can be seen at the temple entrance). There are another two chapels on the second terrace. That on the right, dedicated to Anubis, is adorned with scenes of offerings to Anubis and Amun, their poly-

 Temple of Hatshepsut: columned portico.

The chief of Punt, accompanied by his wife and a nobleman ■ carrying myrrh on a tray. Fragment from the second terrace in the Temple of Hatshepsut, Egyptian Museum of Cairo.

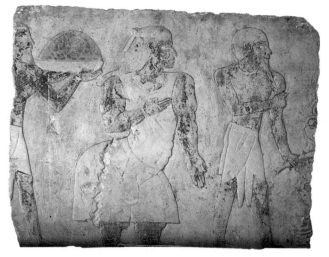

chrome well conserved. The chapel on the left, dedicated to Hathor, features columns with Hathor capitals as in the Temple of Dendera. Finally, the third terrace contains statues of the queen and scenes showing carriers of offerings, all going towards the sanctuary, which is partially excavated into the rock.

The ruins which stand to the left of the Temple of Hatshepsut are those of the **temple and tomb of Mentuhotep I**, an 11th Dynasty Pharaoh.

■ Temple of Hatshepsut: view of the Chapel of Anubis with scenes showing offerings to Anubis and Amun.

Two views of the Temple of Seti I. ■

Mortuary Temple of Seti I in Dra Abu El-Naga

This was one of the largest mortuary temples of Egypt, but we cannot now appreciate its immense size, as the pylons have been lost. Construction began under Seti I and was completed by his son, Ramses II. The temple is dedicated to Seti I, the triad of Thebes and Osiris.

The Ramesseum.

The Ramesseum

The Mortuary Temple of Ramses II is better known as the Ramesseum, as it was named by the French oriental scholar Jean-François Champollion. The temple follows the classical design, with two pylons, though the first is now in very poor condition. Both pylons are decorated with scenes from the famous Battle of Kadesh against the Hittites, though the second pylon also features scenes from the feast of the god Min. All these conserve remains of the original polychrome. Standing beside the second pylon is the largest colossus ever carved by man, though now in ruins, and which must have weighed some 1,000 tons. The hypostyle hall is like that at Karnak, with two central rows of columns, the taller ones with open papyriform capitals, the lower ones with closed papyriform capitals, creating windows that can still be seen. The columns in the next room are lower, with lotiform capitals that still conserve part of their original polychrome. The antechamber ceiling is decorated with interesting astrological scenes.

The adobe buildings behind the temple were used for storage.

Columns in the Ramesseum.

Aerial view of Medinet Habu. ■

Medinet Habu

Medinet Habu is a site containing several temples, impressive due to its shape, size and degree of conservation. The greater part of the site is occupied by the Mortuary Temple of Ramses III, who also built the adobe walls around the complex with its castle-style entrance, influenced by Syrian architecture and adorned with typical scenes showing the offering of war captives to Amun-Ra.

The site, known since the 18th Dynasty, formed part of the Feast of the Valley route, when the statue of Amun was left here for a few days, for which reason Hatshepsut and Thutmosis III built the **Temple of Amun** which stands on the right as we enter. To the left are the ruined chapels of the divine adoratrices of Amun (25th and 26th Dynasties).

The **Mortuary Temple of Ramses III** is the best-conserved of all. The first pylon features scenes representing, on one side, the Pharaoh offering his enemies to Amun, and, on the other side, to Ra. From this pylon, we enter the first court with, on the right, pillars with figures of Ramses in the form of Osiris and, on the left, columns with lotiform capitals. The walls are adorned with war scenes.

Temple of Medinet Habu: Pharaoh Ramses III before Amun. ■

A smaller pylon separates this court from the next where, on one side, are scenes from Ramses III's famous war against the so-called "sea peoples" and, on the other, celebration of the feast of Amun-Min.

113

■ Temple of Medinet Habu: relief representing a wild bull hunt.

■ Temple of Medinet Habu: ceiling over the entrance to the second courtyard.

Temple of Medinet Habu: view of the columns.

On either side of the ruined hypostyle hall in this temple are ten chapels devoted to such deities as Osiris and Ptah.

Outside the temple, on the north wall, are scenes depicting the first naval battle in history, that between Ramses III and the "sea peoples". To the south are the ruins of the royal palace where the Pharaoh no doubt resided when he visited the site.

The Colossi of Memnon

The most magnificent mortuary temple that ever existed was that of Amenophis III. This, unfortunately, is now lost, but the colossal statues that once flanked its doors are conserved. Carved in red quartz, these 18 metres high statues are better known as the Colossi of Memnon. The statues represented the seated Pharaoh with two female figures by his legs: his wife and his mother.

The name Memnon was given to these statues by the Greeks when, due to a terrible earthquake that struck Egypt in 27 BC, the north statue became cracked. Passing through these cracks, the wind produced a pleasant tolling sound, particularly at around daybreak. This sparked the popular belief that this was the god Memnon singing to welcome his mother, Aurora. Many Greeks and Romans visited the site to witness this marvel, but after restoration work carried out under Septimius Severus (emperor from 193 to 211 AD), that marvellous sound was heard no more.

The Colossi of Memnon.

■ Temple of Esna.

■ Temple of Esna: view of the reliefs on the columns.

The city of **Esna** lies 55 kilometres south of Luxor and is a regular stopping-place for boats travelling along the Nile, which have to pass through a lock here. It was in Esna that the Ancient Egyptians worshipped a fish, *Lates Niloticus*, and indeed the Greeks knew the city as Latopolis. Esna's most important monument is a temple built during the Graeco-Roman period and dedicated to Khnum, the potter god. All that remains of the temple, however, is the hypostyle hall, located 9 metress below ground level in a city square. This hall, one of the most beautiful in Egypt, has 24 columns, with composite capitals, adorned with offering scenes and hieroglyphics about the 211 feasts celebrated every year in Esna. On the walls are representations of Ptolemies and Roman emperors from the 2nd century BC to the 3rd century AD, and a mysterious script featuring crocodile and ram hieroglyphs. The ceiling is decorated too, with zodiac signs and astrological scenes reminiscent of the ceiling at Dendera.

El **Kab**, originally Nekhab, the ancient capital of Upper Egypt where the Nekhbet, goddess of the south, represented as a vulture, was worshipped. All that remains of the ancient city are the ruins of the walls and of the temples devoted to Thoth and to Nekhbet built in Roman times.

A little to the north is the necropolis, containing tombs cut into the rock during the Middle and New Kingdom periods. Particularly interesting is the Tomb of Prince Amosis, son of Ibana, who took part in the Egyptian wars against the Hyksos.

Temple of Esna: columns in ■
the hypostyle hall.

EDFU

■ Temple of Edfu: temple guards.

Edfu boasts the best-conserved temple in all Egypt. Built of sandstone between 237 and 57 BC on the remains of an older, New Kingdom temple, this temple stands on a site where, according to Egyptian mythology, one of the battles between Horus the Elder and Set took place. It is dedicated to the god Horus, "Eduf's greatest god" who forms a triad with his wife, Hathor, and his son, Ihy.

The building takes the classical form of the Egyptian temple, beginning with a monumental pylon adorned with scenes showing Ptolemy XII killing his enemies before Horus. This gives entry into a large, well-conserved courtyard surrounded by a colonnade of composite columns. On either side of the entrance are scenes depicting the feast celebrating the anniversary of Horus and Hathor, when the goddess was brought from her temple in Dendera to visit her husband. At the end of this courtyard is finely-made and well-proportioned sculpture of a falcon, the sacred bird of Horus.

The first hypostyle hall, with its tall columns, was decorated with interesting reliefs, though these were later erased by the Christians who lived in the temple. The second hypostyle hall features scenes of the construction and dedication of the temple, and of the feast of the reunion with the sun, when the statue of Horus was taken from the sanctuary and left under the sun for a whole day,

Statue of Horus. ■

118

Temple of Edfu: first hypostyle hall.

Temple of Edfu: second hypostyle hall.

in order to become recharged with its energy. Inside the sanctuary, at the end of the temple, is the naos or tabernacle, carved from a solid block of black granite and weighing nearly 57 tons, before which is the altar. Finally, there are several chambers around and behind the temple that were used to keep objects used in the ceremonies. Outside the temple are the remains of a smaller building. This is the mammisi, usually built in Graeco-Roman times to celebrate the birth of the son of the god or goddess to whom the temple is dedicated.

Temple of Edfu: sanctuary.

KOM OMBO

■ Temple of Kom Ombo: remains of the temple dedicated to the gods Sobek and Haroeris.

The Temple of **Kom Ombo**, which lies between Edfu and Aswan, was built in sandstone by the Ptolemies on the site an earlier temple dating back to the time of the Pharaohs, and was completed by the Romans. This is a double temple, divided longways into two parts, each devoted to a different deity: the left side to Haroeris (a form of Horus), with his falcon's head; the right side to Sobek, god of agriculture, represented with a crocodile's head. The temple follows the traditional ground plan, but has only a single pylon. The courtyard leads to two hypostyle halls and three antechambers leading to the two gods' respective sanctuaries. The scenes decorating the temple depict offerings for the most part, but there are two very interesting other scenes. One, in the first antechamber, is concerned with the temple's festive calendar, showing the 192 feasts that were celebrated every year in Kom Ombo, whilst the other includes representations of surgical instruments before Imhotep, god of medicine.

Outside the temple, on the right, is a chapel dedicated to Hathor containing crocodile mummies. On the left lie the remains of the temple mammisi and a Nilometer, its well connected to the Nile, used to measure the level of the river's waters.

■ Temple of Kom Ombo: hypostyle hall.

Temple of Kom Ombo: relief of the festive calendar. ■

■ Temple of Kom Ombo: relief of a goddess.

Temple of Kom Ombo: reliefs of surgical instruments. ■

ASWAN

■ Aswan. Feluccas on the Nile.

■ Mausoleum of the Aga Khan.

Aswan is one of the most beautiful cities in Egypt. Here the eye can feast on the bright green of the vegetation, the yellow of the sand and the blue of the sky and the Nile, dotted with the white sails of the faluccas that rock gently on its waters, as the river has all the serenity of a lake here. Today's Aswan is a modern city with 200,000 inhabitants. Its ancient name is Senyt, from which the present name is derived, and this was the principal city in the south of the country, lying by the first cataract of the Nile, which separated Egypt from neighbouring Nubia. Facing city, on the west bank, are the **rock-cut tombs** where the nobles of Aswan were buried in the times of the Pharaohs. Particularly interesting are those of Harkhof and Sarenput. Further south is the **Mausoleum of the Aga Khan**, Imam of the Ismaeli Muslims, buried here in 1957. The city also overlooks Kitchener's Island, known as the beautiful **Botanical Garden of Aswan**, with its many different species of tropical plants.

Nevertheless, the main attraction in Aswan is, without doubt, **Elephantine Island**, which takes its name from the shape of the granite rocks in the south of the island. This is where we find the ruins of the **Temple of Khnum**, the potter god. Aswan's most important temple, it goes back to the times of the Old Kingdom, but was later rebuilt by several Pharaohs during the Middle and New Kingdom periods, and by the Ptolemies. Beside the temple is a **Nilometer**, of vital importance in ancient times, as it was used to gauge the river rise and so predict the harvest.

In the afternoon, the view of the sunset over this island from the terrace of the **Hotel Old Cataract** is one of the most unforgettable in the country. The hotel itself is no less interesting, as it is housed in an early-20th-century royal palace.

Aswan is very lively at night, particularly in summer, when there is some respite from the stifling heat of the day. The most popular areas are the *Corniche* sea front promenade, Market Street and Railway Station Square.

South of Aswan is the **quarry** whose granite was used to make obelisks and other monolithic ele-

View of the Botanical Garden of Aswan from the Nile. ■

ments. Here we can see the **unfinished obelisk**, which was not finally taken from the site as cracks had appeared in the block. If not, this would have been the largest obelisk of all: 42 metres high, weighing 1,176 tons.

Further south, at the head of the cataract, the British built a **dam** in 1902. Over time, though, this dam became too small, and President Nasser ordered a larger one built in 1960. The **High Dam**, which is 17 times the size of the Cheops Pyramid, was finally opened in 1971 forming Lake Nasser further south. With a total length of some 500 km, this is the second largest artificial lake in the world, providing water for irrigation throughout the year and generating the electricity needed to industrialise the country.

The Hotel Old Cataract from the Nile. ■

Aswan market: stalls selling spices and nargiles.

The Great Aswan Dam.

The unfinished obelisk in the quarry at Aswan.

PHILAE

■ The Temple of Philae from the Nile.

The temples which once stood on the island of **Philae**, which was submerged under the waters of the Nile by the construction of the Aswan Dam, were transported stone by stone to the nearby island of Agilkia. This huge rescue operation, carried out by UNESCO between 1972 and 1980, after moving several temples in Lower Nubia. Philae's main temple is dedicated to the goddess Isis, her husband, Osiris, and her son, Horus. Construction of this sandstone monument began under Nektanebo

■ Temple of Philae: columns.

First pylon at the Temple of Philae. ■

II, the last Egyptian Pharaoh (4th century BC), and was completed by the Ptolemies, though additions were also made in the Roman period. Entrance to the temple is from the landing quay, beside which stand the ruins of the Pavilion of Nektanebo. A row of columns leads to the first pylon, featuring scenes showing Ptolemy XII before Isis and marked by graffiti left by Napoleonic troops. This first pylon leads to a courtyard in which, on the left, is the temple mammisi. A second pylon leads to the hypostyle hall, which was converted into a church in Christian times. Passing through several antechambers, we come to the sanctuary, whose side chambers are adorned with fine reliefs. Generally speaking, as we can see from drawings made by 19th century painters, all the reliefs in this temple conserve most of their polychrome.

Several buildings stand beside the Temple of Isis: a smaller temple, dedicated to Hathor, in which there

Trajan's Kiosk. ■

is a representation of the goddess Hathor with Bes, god of joy, playing musical instruments; a tall chapel known as Trajan's Kiosk, its columns sporting lovely composite capitals; and the remains of a church built in the 6th century AD.

LOWER NUBIA

■ The Nile and the desert at the start of the Nubian region.

South of Aswan lies **Nubia**, whose name derives from the hieroglyphic word "nub-gold". The region was indeed rich in gold, and the Egyptian kings came here in search of it. Made part of the empire, the region was divided

■ Typical Nubian house.

■ Interior of a Nubian house.

Nubian women bathing in the Nile. ■

in two: Lower Nubia, between the first and second cataracts of the Nile, that is, from Aswan almost to Egypt's frontier with Sudan, and Upper Nubia, from the second cataract to the fourth, now part of Sudan.

The construction of the High Dam and Lake Nasser forced some 65,000 Nubians to emigrate to areas around Aswan, where the Egyptian government built them settlements with houses that respect their traditional lifestyle. The Nubian people also conserve

Lake Nasser. ▨

Temple of Kalabsha: relief of the god Mandolis.

Temple of Kalabsha: first courtyard.

the temples of Kalabsha, Qertas and El-Wali; the second, 140 km to the south, near Sebuak, the temples of Wadi El-Sebu, Dakka and Maharraqua; the third, around half-way along the lake, the temples of Amada and Derr and the tomb of Penut; and the fourth, some 260 km south of Aswan, the Abu Simbel complex.

Kalabsha, Qertas and Beit El-Wali

The Temple of Kalabsha is one of the largest in Nubia. It was built by the Emperor Augustus in the 1st century BC and is dedicated to the god Mendolis, a local form of Horus. It consists of a pylon, a courtyard, a hypostyle hall and the sanctuary, though many of the reliefs are unfinished.

Qertas is a small chapel, also built during the Roman period. The fine columns are adorned, some with floral motifs, others with Hathor capitals.

The Temple of Beit El-Wali was built by Ramses II and is dedicated to Amun and other deities, including Isis, Horus and Khnum. The courtyard walls of this temple, which is partially excavated into the mountain, are decorated with scenes depicting Ramses II fighting against his enemies, whilst the reliefs inside the temple show the Pharaoh making offerings to different gods.

their own oral dialect, though they also speak Arabic. In 1960, to save the Lower Nubian monuments situated in the dam and lake construction area, UNESCO made a worldwide call for help and these were moved to higher ground, grouped into four areas: the first, near the High Dam, includes

Temple of Qertas.

Temple of Beit El-Wali: detail of the relief depicting one of the battles of Ramses II. ▪

■ Temple of Wadi El-Sebu: view of the sphinxes at the temple entrance.

Wadi El-Sebu, Dakka and Maharraqua

The Temple of Wadi El-Sebu, meaning Valley of the Lions, takes its name from the sphinxes that stand at the entrance. The temple was built by Ramses II using local sandstone and is dedicated, like most temples in Nubia, to Amun and Ra. It consists of three pylons followed by a hypostyle hall with twelve columns, an antechamber and the sanctuary, which was later converted into a Christian church.

The temple in Dakka is dedicated to Thoth. It was built by Arkamani in around 220 BC, though it also features additions and decorative elements from the Ptolemaic and Roman periods.

The unfinished Temple of Maharraqua dates back to Roman times and is dedicated to Serapis.

Amada, Derr and the Tomb of Penut

The temple of Amada, dedicated to Amun and Ra, is the oldest in Nubia, as it was built by Thutmose III and Amenophis II, although extended under Thutmose IV, Seti I and Ramses II. The colours of the reliefs have been very well conserved. This is the

■ Temple of Dakka.

only temple to be transferred whole, without cutting into blocks like the others.

Derr is a temple very similar to that of Abu Simbel. Partially excavated into the mountain, it was built by Ramses II and is dedicated to Ptah, Amun, Ramses II and Ra.

The decoration of the Tomb of Penut, a high-ranking official under Ramses VI, has been well conserved, with scenes showing Penut worshipping or making offerings to various deities.

Nubian guard at the Temple of Amada. ■

■ Temple of Wadi El-Sebu: detail of a sphinx.

■ Temple of Dakka: relief of the goddess Anket.

Entrance to the Tomb of Pennut. ■

 The Great Temple of Ramses II.

■ View of the Abu Simbel monumental site with its two temples.

Abu Simbel

Abu Simbel is the name of the mountain into which two temples dedicated to Ramses II were excavated into the rock. The site rose to fame due to the risky operation launched to prevent them from being submerged under water due to the construction of Lake Nasser. This delicate operation, carried out by UNESCO between 1964 and 1968, consisted in cutting both temples into a total of 807 blocks and reconstructing them 65 metres higher and 235 metress inland from their original emplacement, after which they were covered by concrete domes cased in rock and sand.

The **Great Temple of Ramses II** is the most important monument in Nubia. It is excavated some 48 metress into the mountain, its facade made up of four 20 metres high colossus of Ramses II. Over the entrance are two reliefs of Ramses making offerings to Ra, above which are the Pharaoh's titles. The first hall contains eight pillars, each adorned with a figure of the Pharaoh in the form of Osiris.

One of the four colossal sculptures representing Ramses II, and a sculpture of Nefertari. ■

Great Temple of
Ramses II: first
room.

Interior of the
sanctuary in the
Temple of Ramses II,
where on just two
days a year the first
rays of the son bathe
the three gods here,
except Ptah (the god
of the underworld),
who remains in
shadow.

Great Temple of Ramses II: partial view of a relief in the first room, representing Ramses II slaying his enemies with his mace. ■

■ Great Temple of Ramses II: reliefs with warlike scenes in the first room.

■ Great Temple of Ramses II: reliefs in the second room.

Entrance to the Temple of Nefertari. ■

The walls on the right are adorned with scenes representing the Battle of Kadesh against the Hittites, and the other walls also feature war scenes. The second chamber is smaller, with just four pillars. Here we see scenes of the Pharaoh before the sacred barques of Amun and Ra. Finally, the sanctuary contains four statues, of Ptah, Amun, Ramses II and Ra, to whom the temple is dedicated. This is the only room in the temple that is visited by the sun's rays, which recharge these gods with energy. The mountain is perforated so that this occurs just twice a year, on February 22 and October 22, and in such a way that Ptah, the god of the underworld, is not illuminated.

The other temple on Abu Simbel, smaller, is dedicated to Hathor and Queen **Nefertari**. Its façade is composed of six statues: three on either side of the entrance, each group comprising two statues of Ramses II and, between them, one of his wife, Nefertari, in the form of Hathor. The hypostyle hall as six Hathor columns, the walls decorated with scenes showing the Pharaoh and Nefertari making offerings to the gods. At the end of the temple, the sanctuary contains a statue of the goddess Hathor, though in much deteriorated condition.

Temple of Nefertari. ■

EL FAYUM

■ Crops at El-Fayum.

The province of **el Fayum** is the Egypt's largest oasis, and the one nearest to Cairo. Lying some 100 km southwest of the capital, it has a population of more than one million inhabitants.

The zone, inhabited since the early days of the Pharaohs, acquired particular importance during the Middle Kingdom, when such Pharaohs as Amenemhat III carried out irrigation projects here in order to cultivate the land, building temples such

■ Ruins of the Temple of Medinet Madi.

as that of **Medinet Madi**. The Ptolemies also prizes these lands, building small cities and many temples here, the remains of which are found all over the province.

The provincial capital, **Medinet el Fayum**, with nearly 280,000 inhabitants, is famed for its waterwheels, some driven by canals, others by spa water sources. North of the city lies **Lake Karun**, 44 metres below sea level. The lake is 50 x 12 kilometress in size, its depth ranging between 4 and 18 metress. This is an ideal place for fishing and birdwatching, and is a popular destination, particularly in winter, for many from the Egyptian capital, who flock here to enjoy a relaxing holiday.

South of El Fayum is the **pyramid of Hauara**, built by Amenemhat III in adobe brick, covered in stone. The entrance is on the south side. According to classical historians, the mortuary temple that once stood beside the temple had two storeys, each with 1,500 rooms, for which reason it was known as "the labyrinth". Also in the south is the **pyramid of El-Lahun**, built by Senwosret III and very similar to that of Hauara, also made from adobe brick covered with stone.

Waterwheels.

■ Lake Karun.

Pyramid of Hauara. ■

THE OASES

■ Oasis of Bahariya.

The province known as New Valley, in the Western Desert, contains Egypt's oases, the largest of them **El-Kharga**, which lies on the same latitude as Edfu, stretching for nearly 100 km to the north. The city of El-Kharga, ancient Hibis to the Greeks, contains the 4th-century BC Temple of Hibis, dedicated to Amun. North of the city is the Christian necropolis of El-Bagawat, which dates to the 5th century. Also interesting, 32 km north of the city, are the remains of the Temple of Qasr El-Ghueita, dedicated to the Theban triad.

The oasis of **Dakhla**, whose capital is Mut, does not offer such variety. The main monument here are the Roman tombs in El-Muzawaqa, which conserve their bright colours, particularly those of Petosiris and Petubastis.

El-Bahariya. The 26th-Dynasty tombs found near

■ Oasis of Bahariya: insemination of palm trees.

Oasis of Bahariya: craft shop. ■

Oasis of Bahariya: two views of the tomb of Bannentoi.

■ Views of the White Desert, whose limestone rock formations, shaped by wind erosion, form one of the most unusual landscapes in Egypt.

■ View of the Black Desert.

Overall view of the Oasis of Siwa. ■

the capital, Bawiti, are, along with the so-called Valley of the Golden Mummies, the most important sights in this oasis. However, we should also mention the sulphurous spa water sources found all over the oasis. Both **El-Bahariya** and **Farafra** oases are surrounded by the fascinating black, white and glassy deserts.

Finally, the main attraction at the oasis of **Siwa**, near the frontier with Libya, is formed by the ruins of the Temple of Amun, built in around 550 BC.

Oasis of Siwa: ruins of the Temple of the Oracle of Amun, where Alexander the Great was crowned. ■

ALEXANDRIA

Alexandria is today Egypt's second most important city, with a population of over three million inhabitants. When Alexander the Great ordered the construction of a new capital of the country he had just conquered (332 BC), there was just a fishing village named Racotis here. Charged by Alexander to draw up plans for the new city, Dinocrates of Rhodes, the arquitect, connected Racotis to the island facing it, Pharos, by a dyke, forming two harbours. He designed a rectangular-shaped city, with two main roads that crossed where the Royal Palace and other important buildings stood. Dying in 323 BC, Alexander the Great never saw the new city, and Ptolemy I was the first king to live in and rule from Alexandria, whilst his successor, Ptolemy II turned this into the most important city in the Mediterranean, and so it remained until the times of the last monarch in this dynasty, Queen Cleopatra VII.

During the reign of Ptolemy II, Sostratos of Cnidus built the celebrated **Lighthouse of Alexandria** at the easternmost point of the island of Pharos. One of the Seven Wonders of the World, this tower was 120 metress high and supported a huge mirror that could reflect the light of its beacon up to a distance of 150 km over the sea. Unfortunately, the lighthouse was destroyed by several earthquakes, and stones from it were used in medieval times to build **Qaitbay Citadel** to defend the city against attacks by the Crusaders.

Rebuilt in 1982, this fortress now houses a Naval Museum whose collections more than 40,000 pieces were located next to it in the water during submarine archaeological investigations over the last few years. The **Abul-Abas El-Mursi Mosque**, one of the most

 Abul Abas El-Mursi Mosque.

The citadel of Qaitbay. ■

interesting and important in the city, stands near this fortress.

The Museion ("house of wisdom") or University of Alexandria was one of the most important in the world. The famous **Library**, founded by Ptolemy I and enriched by Ptolemy II was particularly remarkable. The task the library's founders set themselves was to purchase original manuscripts from all the sages, or to obtain a copy from them when this was not possible, thus building up the largest and most complete

Alexandria: The Corniche. ■

■ View of the new building that houses the Library of Alexandria.

■ Interior of the Library of Alexandria.

Library of Alexandria: planetarium. ■

library in the world. Unfortunately, it burnt down; in around 49 BC, during the times of Julius Caesar, fire broke out in the harbour, destroying all the ships there but, contrary to many versions, not reaching the Library. Nonetheless, Egypt recently opened the new **Library of Alexandria** thanks to a protocol signed with a UNESCO in 1990 to make this once more a centre for pilgrimages in search of knowledge. The new building, with nine storeys, houses millions of books and countless computers connected to the most important libraries all over the world, as well as an interesting manuscript museum and a planetarium.

The **Serapeum** was the main temple in Alexandria, where the city's most-revered god, Serapis (a mixture of Osiris and Apis), was worshipped, along with his wife, Isis, and his son, Horus the Child. Little has been conserved of the temple however: all that remains on the site is a 30 metres high pink granite column known as Pompeii's Column.

■ Pompeii's Column in the Serapeum.

■ Kom El-Shukafa catacombs: tomb with representations of Egyptian and Greek mythology.

The **Kom El-Shukafa** catacomb is a three-storey underground cemetery dating back to the 1st century AD. The decoration of some of these tombs reveals an interesting mixture of Egyptian and Greek mythology, both in style and subject matter. Other interesting tombs in Alexandria also include those of **Anfushi** and **Mostafa Kamel**.

It is thought that the reduced dimensions of the **Roman Theatre**, built under the Emperor Tiberius (1st century AD), are due to the fact that this was a private

■ Main funerary chamber in the Kom El-Shukafa catacombs.

150

El-Manchia square. ■

theatre built adjoining a palace. Some fine Roman mosaics featuring interesting bird motifs, have been discovered just beside the theatre. More works from this period can also be seen in the **Graeco-Roman Museum**, which houses pieces found both in Alexandria and in other places all over Egypt.

Present-day Alexandria is a city with very much a Mediterranean nature and appearance. The sea front promenade, or **Corniche**, is one of the most beautiful in the country, attracting flocks of visitors from Cairo in summer. It is here that we find the 19th-century **Hotel Cecil**, which evokes the times when many foreigners came here, attracted by Mohammed Ali's work in developing Egyptian industry and trade, making Alexandria a cosmopolitan city. The **Muntazah Palace**, the residence of kings and now the president's summer residence, also dates back to this period. The palace grounds, open to the public, cover an area of 140 hectares. The city centre is now formed by three squares, **Midan Saad Zaghlul**, adjoining the Corniche, **Midan El-Manchia** and **Midan El-Mahatta**. The squares are presided over by statues of leading personalities from Egypt's modern history, and are lined by many bars, fish restaurants and bazaars.

Zanket El-Settat market. ■

THE DELTA

■ The Kanatir Al-Khahireya Dam.

The **Nile Delta** lies just a few kilometress north of Cairo, where the river divides into two arms. This was where Mohammed Ali ordered the construction of the Kanatir Al-Khahireya Dam to control irrigation in the zone. Overall, the delta forms a 22,000 km² triangle of very fertile land thanks to the silt the Nile has carried here over the centuries, enabling this land to be cultivated since the time of the Pharaohs and even today. The main crop in the delta is cotton, whilst rice is the principal product harvested in the north. Divided into several provinces, the delta is home to some 20 million people. The population is concentrated, above all, in the cities of **Tanta**, **Damanhur**, **Mansura** and **Zagazig**. At either end of the Nile's two arms lie the cities of **Rosetta**, to the west, which gives the western arm of the river its name, and **Damietta**, to the east, and which also shares its name with the Nile's eastern arm.

The most important archaeological site in the delta is **Tanis**, near the site of the Egyptian capital under the Hyksos (15th and 16th Dynasties). Later,

■ Rosetta: medieval houses.

Ramses II had a royal residence built in Tanis, and the capital was transferred here once more during the 21st and 22nd Dynasties. Now, however, only ruins remain of a temple, and remains of statues and obelisks. In 1939, several royal tombs were found here, and these are now on show in the Tanis Room in the Egyptian Museum of Cairo.

Archaeological site of Tanis: sculpture of Ramses. ■

Archaeological site of Tanis. ■

153

THE SUEZ CANAL

■ A transatlantic liner passes along the Suez Canal.

According to the chronicles of the Greek historian Strabo, the first Pharaoh to plan a link from the Nile to the Red Sea by a man-made canal which avoided the journey across the desert, was Sesostris in the 20th century BC. Work did not begin, however, until the reign of Nekau II in the 26th Dynasty. in the late-7th century BC, continuing under the Ptolemies. Later, in the 7th century AD, Caliph Omar ordered repairs to be made to the canal, which had become blocked by sediments.

■ Suez: fish market.

Construction of the present **Suez Canal** began in 1859 as a joint project between Egypt and France. The canal was finally opened in 1869 with great celebrations. However, the cost of these celebrations forced Egypt to sell its share in the canal operating company to the British government, which did not miss this chance to interfere in Egypt's political affairs, finally occupying the country in 1882. The Suez Canal remained in British and French hands until 1956, when President Nasser nationalised it.

The Suez Canal is 195 kilometres long, nearly 300 metres wide and 34 metress deep. The canal plays a vitally important strategic role in western trade with Asia, as ships can save the voyage around Africa via the Cape of Good Hope. There is no doubt, moreover, that seeing the great ships sailing through the desert along the canal is one of the most impressive sights in Egypt.

The oldest city in the canal zone is **Suez**, at the southernmost end, established in the 15th century. Besides giving its name to the whole canal, Suez is the most important fishing port in the Red Sea. Two new cities also sprang up due to the construction of the canal: **Port Said**, at the northern end, now an important trading centre, and **Ismailiya**, halfway along the canal, at the point where a small lake opens up, at whose northernmost point are the headquarters of the canal operating company.

Port Said: the Suez Canal Company in the 1920s. ■

Ismailiya: reproduction of the carriage which brought ■
King Ismael to open the Suez Canal.

SINAI

■ Sunset over Sinai.

The name of the **Sinai** Peninsula seems to derive from Sin, the moon god, widely known in the Middle East. The peninsula forms a huge inverted triangle with an area of nearly 61,000 km^2, bordered to the east by the Gulf of Aqaba and Israel, to the west by the Gulf and the Suez Canal, to the north by the Mediterranean Sea and to the south by the Red Sea. The peninsula is divided into two provinces: Shamal Sinai (northern Sinai) and Janub Sinai (southern Sinai).

Northern Sinai

With an area of 27,574 km^2, Shamal Sinai province has a population of nearly 224,000 inhabitants. Most of the territory is occupied by the sandy valley of Al-Arish, with its landscape of dunes. Not far from Ismailiya, the **Firdan bridge** provides communications between northern Sinai and the rest of Egypt. There are two particularly interesting attractions here: Lake Bardawil and the capital, al Arish.

Lake Bardawil lies beside the Mediterranean. The principal economic activity in this area is fishing from

The Firdan bridge. ■

A mountain bathed by sunlight.

■ Al-Arish palm grove.

■ Sunset in Al-Arish: minarets and palms.

the well-stocked waters of this lake. Practically the entire eastern half of the lake is occupied by a protected area, **Zaranik**. In autumn, from October to December, more than 200 species of migratory birds gather here.

Al-Arish is the most highly populated city in Sinai, with 40,000 inhabitants. The resort boasts magnificent beaches, lined by a beautiful palm grove, giving the area its name of the "coast of palms" and mak-ing this the favourite holiday destination of many Egyptians, who have built chalets here.

Southern Sinai

The southern Sinai province has an area of 33,140 km² and a population of 46,000. Access from the continent is by the **Ahmed Hamdi tunnel**, 17 kilometres north of the city of Suez, built between 1975 and 1980. The tunnel is 10.5 metres in diam-

Rock formations in Sinai.

Ruins of the Temple of Serabit Al-Khadem.

eter, 4,500 metres long, 1,700 underground, running 37 metres below the Suez Canal. The most interesting sights in this province are the ruins of the Temple of Serabit Al-Khadem, Saint Catherine's Monastery, Mount Moses, the city of Sharm El-Sheikh and the Ras Muhammad nature reserve.

It was Snefru, the first Pharaoh of the 4th Dynasty, who ordered the construction of the **Temple of Serabit Al-Khadem**, dedicated to the goddess Hathor, partially excavated into the rock. Later, other Pharaohs, particularly during the 18th Dynasty, extended the site with new chambers supported by square columns adorned with the head of Hathor. As also occurred with the engraved stones from the **Maghara turquoise mines**, which lie near the temple, several of the reliefs that decorated its walls have been taken to the Egyptian Museum in Cairo. These reliefs depict different expeditions sent out by the Pharaohs.

St Catherine's is an important religious site as it contains Mount Horeb, which is where Moses heard the voice of God in the burning bush. Saint Catherine's Monastery was later built on the same site, according to the reliefs over the door, in 557, by the Emperor Justinian. Nevertheless, earlier, in 377 AD, Saint Helena had ordered the construction of a small chapel over the roots of the sacred bush, and this still stands. In the monastery, protected by a high wall and currently inhabited by some 20 monks, the most interesting elements are the Byzantine-style church, the library and the collection of more than 2,000 icons from different periods that are found all over the site.

Near the monastery stand **Mount Catherine** (Gabal Katerina), at 2,642 metres the highest in Egypt, and **Mount Moses** (Gabal Musa), which rises to a height of 2,285 metres. The latter is the holiest place in Sinai, as this was where Moses received the Ten Commandments. There are two paths to the peak from Saint Catherine's Monastery; a staircase with 3,750 steps built by the monks, and the path made by Abbas I, king of Egypt, in the early-20th century. This second route

Saint Catherine's Monastery.

 Saint Catherine's Monastery: Chapel of the Burning Bush, basilica nave and apse.

■ The coloured canyon.

consists of a series of ramps followed by around 700 steps going up to the tiny plateau on the mountain-top, where a chapel dedicated to the Holy Trinity stands. The views from this peak are magnificent, particular at sunrise and sunset.

Sharm El-Sheikh is the most important city in the Gulf of Aqaba, and a veritable paradise, attracting many tourists to spend their holidays here. The most attractive resort area is Sharm el Sheikh, a few kilometres to the north. Known as **Nema Bay**, this is where we find the main hotels, bars and restaurants. By day, visitors enjoy the fantastic sandy beaches and turquoise waters, whilst in the evening the bars provide a lively nightlife, though all hotels also have their own regular programmes of shows.

Ras Muhammad lies near Sharm El-Sheikh, at the southernmost point of the Sinai Peninsula, where the currents from the gulfs of Suez and Aqaba meet. Due to the importance of its marine heritage, this natural jewel in Sinai's crown was declared Egypt's first protected area in 1983. The natural reserve now covers an area of 480 km².

Sharm El-Sheikh. ■

St Anthony's Monastery: view of the frescoes on the walls of the Chapel of St Anthony. ■

St Paul's Monastery. ■

Two views of Hurghada.

Red Sea fish: clownfish *(Amphiprion bicinctus)*, Napoleon fish
(Cheilinus undulatus), fusilier fish *(Caesionidae sp.)*, coral cod
(Cephalopholis miniata) and Red Sea angelfish *(Pomacanthus*
maculosus).

A shoal of Anthias (*Anthias squamipinnis*).

Blue spotted stingray (*Taeniura lymma*).

Denizens of the coral reef.

■ Hawksbill sea turtle (*Eretmochelys imbricata*) and crab.

of the Red Sea coast. It is equally very attractive for lovers of marine life, so that it is expected to grow as big as Hurghada soon.

Indeed, words cannot describe the wonders of the Red Sea, the sensations one enjoys when immersing oneself in its waters and contemplating this incredible underwater world. For this reason, we prefer to present it in this book through images and complement them with a map of the most recommended areas for diving.

■ Red Sea coral: "soft coral" (*Tubastrea sp.*), "hard coral" and Red Sponge (*Latrunculia corticata*).

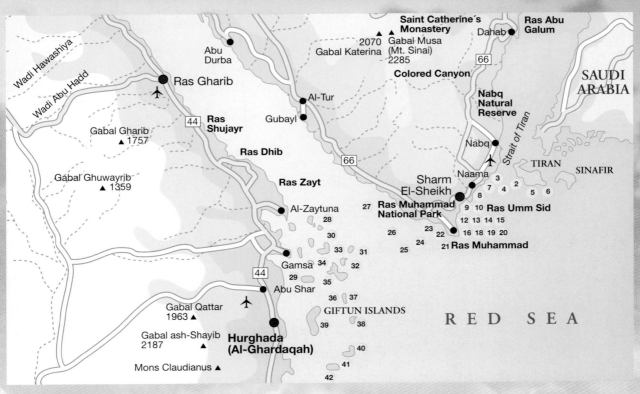

DIVING AREAS OF THE RED SEA

1. Small Lagoon. Shallow reef but with strong currents. Moorings available. Area of pelagic fish and remains of the shipwreck "Sangria".

2. Large Lagoon. Shallow reef with coral and sandfish.

3. Jackson Reef. Very shallow reef (70 m), with a large plateau at about 15 m, and dangerous currents. Area of pelagic fish and sharks, and remains of the shipwreck "Lara".

4. Gordon Reef. At a depth of 10-20 m, stretches a wall that goes down 70 m. Strong currents. Area of open sea fish and sharks, and remains of the shipwreck "Loullia".

5. Hushasha. Shallow reef with 12 to 15-m walls. Sandy floor.

6. Abu Tinum. Reef with grottoes and sandy floor. Area of seahorses and, occasionally, sharks.

7. Ras Nasrani (The Lighthouse). Reef of about 40 m in depth and strong currents. Area of pelagic fish.

8. Ras Nasrani (The Point). Area of rocks and hard coral with groupers and coral fish.

9. Shark Bay. Small canyon of 10 to 25 m in length and wall.

10. Far Garden. Wall of 50 m in depth with shallow grottoes (between 5-12 m) and large projections (at 40 m).

11. Near Garden. Reef of 30 m in depth.

12. The Tower. Wall of 60 m in depth

with large grottoes with an outlet to the base of the reef.

13. Amphorae. Sandy floor at 25 m in depth and a small wall. Wreckage of a Turkish boat from the 16th century, which carried mercury, part of which still shines on some coral.

14. Ras Um Sid. Gentle slope with, at about 25 m in depth, large gorgonias and coral. Area of barracuda, rays and, occasionally, sharks.

15. The Temple. Three large pinnacles that rise 20 m from the sandy floor up to the surface.

16. Ras Aslani. Large formations of coral and pelagic fish.

17. Hashabey. Sandy lagoon with coral wall and an enormous grotto at about 25 m in depth.

18. Ras Za'atir. Steep slope down to 50 m in depth. Shallow grottoes, large gorgonias and pelagic fish.

19. Fisherman's Bank. Reef with coral at 25 m in depth. Area of coral fish.

20. Shark Observatory. Famous wall with vertical drops from the surface down to 90 m in depth. Area of pelagic fish and sharks.

21. Shark Reef. Two "islands" on a gentle, sandy slope. Strong currents. Area of open sea fish and sharks.

22. The Quay. Steep slope with coral. Area of pelagic fish and, occasionally, sharks.

23. The Alternatives. Large area with many interesting areas for immersion: small walls, coral and coral fish.

24. The Mushroom. A large pinnacle and, at about 20 m in depth, remains of a shipwreck.

25. Beacon Rock. Steep slope with coral. Area of groupers and sharks. At about 30 m are the remains of the shipwreck "Dunraven" (1876), steam and sail boat that was used for transporting spices and wood.

26. Small Crack. Sandy lagoon cut into a canal. Area of strong currents with soft coral.

27. Shag Rock. Wall of about 25 m with coral and pelagic fish. Area of strong currents. In the northern part is the wreckage of the "Thistlegorm", military supply boat sunk by German bombing in 1941.

28. Bluff Point. Wall of about 20 m and remains of three shipwrecks, two of them in the windward side.

29. Tawila Island. On its southern side, stretches a large coral area with sandy floors. On the island, pools created by the tide.

30. Umn Usk. Wall of about 30 m with large coral formations, the soft coral on the southwest side stands out.

31. Abu Nuhas. Area of strong swells. Underwater, a gentle slope of about 25 m in depth holds the remains of four shipwrecks: on the northeasta point are the "Chrisoula K" and the "Giannis D", two cargo boats that sank in 1981 and 1983; in the middle is the "Carnatic", steam boat that sank in 1869, and the fourth is situated in the southwest part.

32. The Pillars. Various coral pinna-

cles that emerge from the sandy floor at 25 m in depth up to the surface.

33. Blind Reef. Wall of about 25 m with interesting coral formations on the east side.

34. Siyul Kabhira. Reef of 25 m in depth with a platform at 15 m that houses various grottoes in the northwest side.

35. Siyul Saghira. Extensive area of coral formations and a small 20-m wall inside the lagoon.

36. Sha'ab El Erg. Reef in the shape of a horseshoe with abundant coral. Area of pelagic fish and rays.

37. Umm Qamar. 45-m wall with many grottoes and drops, an enormous grotto of about 25 m in depth stands out. Area of coral fish, groupers and, occasionally, sharks.

38. Sha'ab Sagir Umm Qamar. 30-m slope with coral grottoes. Area of pelagic fish, groupers, tunas and barracudas.

39. Careless Reef. Gentle slope downs to a large plateau at about 20 m with a depth of 50 m. Area of large gorgonias and black coral, coral fish and morays.

40. Little Giftun. Wall that in its eastern side is over 60 m in depth, and with a large sandy plateau at 25 m. Area of groupers.

41. Abu Rimata. Wall of great depth (between 20 and 80 m) with numerous grottoes and projections. Area of strong currents.

42. Ata Abu Rimata. Sandy floor reef with shallow coral (about 12 m). Area of coral fish.

THE PEOPLE AND THEIR CUSTOMS

Al Azhar Mosque.

■ Cairoans strolling and sitting at a terrace in the Citadel.

some place is, they don't only tell you, they take you there.

The animated places of the Cairoans are often found in the open air, above all, around the Nile, and summer nights are especially lively. You can see how the boys go out in small groups holding hands, just like the girls or couples, while the vendors of refreshments, grilled corn and lupine stroll among the people in order to sell their products.

Carrot seller in Giza. ■

The Egyptian people are very friendly and hospitable. For this reason, they say that Egypt has a very valuable treasure, its people. Walking through the streets of Cairo, men, women and children look at you with a natural smile, they greet you and when you ask them where

Garlic seller at Cairo's garlic and onion market. ■

Lupin seller in Cairo. ■

■ Delta farmer.

A musician playing the rababa. ■

■ The donkey is a faithful helper in the fields.

The turkey with its owner on a motorbike. ■

The Sun Café. ■

El-Fishawy ■
Café.

Children in a in cart in the delta area.

Cutting sugar cane at El-Minia.

The typical bars, where Cairoans go to have a cup of tea, smoke their shisha (water pipe) and play backgammon, are almost always full. The owners of these bars try to make each one of their locales a place with a very characteristic and special style.

The main festivals for Muslims (85% percent of the population) are the Festival of the Lamb, which lasts four days, and the Bayram coming right after the month of Ramadan, when Muslims fast during the day and take advantage of the night to eat, drink and go out for a walk. During this month, the streets are more lit than usual. Visiting Cairo during Ramadan is really much more impressive. Christmas and Easter are celebrated just like in other countries. There are various national celebrations, among which is October 6, the date of Egypt's victory over Israel in 1973, and July 23, the day of Nasser's Revolution, when Egypt changed from a monarchy to a republic.

There are also festivals of Pharaonic origin like the Day of Spring (Sham El-Nesim), when Egyptians go out at the break of dawn for enjoying the beauty of nature and it is customary to eat vegetables and fish. Gratitude for the Nile (Wafa El-Nil) is a very special festival; celebrated on the Nile with a multitude of decorated boats and flowers.

Weddings in Cairo are very interesting. Their form and colour vary depending upon the purchasing power of the bride and groom, ranging from those celebrated in hotels to those held in the street itself. A week after children are born, their parents celebrate a familial party at home after the first week (a custom from Pharaonic times) and they invite neighbours and relatives, giving them presents with babies' name and date of birth.

Egyptian wedding: the groom's hand with that of the bride's father under the white cloth formalises the marriage. ■

Celebration of "Sebuo", which takes place one week after a baby is born. ■

CRAFTS

■ Stall selling sweets and dolls in Giza.

Alabaster craftsmen, and a potter. ■

In Egypt, watching how the craftsmen work with primitive techniques and create wonders attracts a lot of attention. If it weren't for the heat or the noise, their workshops would appear to be authentic museums or galleries of art. It's possible to buy crafts in all the small markets and tourist centres, and the price is always haggled.

Traditional papyrus of distinct qualities and prices are best bought in the so-called Papyrus Institutes in order to assure that they are made and painted by hand, even though they are copies. A good place is the shops on the Avenue of the Pyramids.
Turquoise and other precious stones are sold by themselves or together with silver and gold jewellery. The

■ Papyrus.

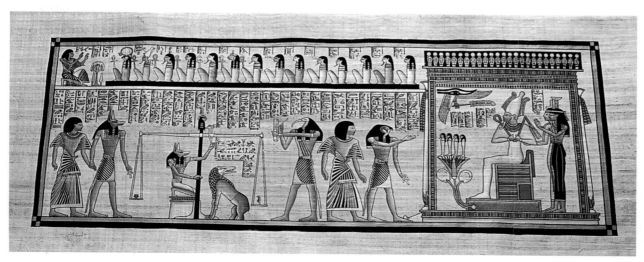

 Tapestry market in Cairo.

Pharaonic rolls, with the name of the person written on them in hieroglyphic characters, are a good souvenir too. In the tapestry and rug schools near Saqqara, fabrics with very original rural motifs are produced. They are made by young boys, who choose the designs themselves.

Egyptian cotton, of very good quality, is very famous.

Visitors to Egypt usually always take galabeya (hooded cloaks), turbans or T-shirts with Egyptian motifs back with them as souvenirs.

Glass blown and painted by hand is a specialty in Cairo. The most abundant articles are the small bottles of perfume in different colours mixed with the colour gold.

Young people making
a tapestry in
Saqqara. ■

Perfume shop. ■

GASTRONOMY

■ Stalls selling fruit in a Cairo market.

Egyptian cuisine is very varied. One of its main bases is vegetables. Because of this, the markets in Cairo and cities all around the country are very interesting. In them, it is possible to find every kind of vegetable, as well as Mediterranean and tropical fruit like mango and guava. Pita bread is a delicacy, besides being a staple food of Egyptians

■ Stalls selling spices.

Stand selling ful (broad beans). ■

Typical food

-**El-Ful** (broad beans). This is the main plate for breakfast and is commonly eaten in pita bread sandwiches with a little bit of salad. It is found at the best restaurants or street-side vendors.

-**Falafel** (croquets of broad beans and vegetables). This is the second most-typical food for breakfast, although it is also eaten at lunch or dinner. It is often eaten with tahina (sesame sauce) and salad.

-**Kochary** (mixed dish of rice, pasta, lentils and onion and tomato sauce). Kochary is eaten in restaurants that only serve this dish.

-**Molukheyaa** (vegetable soup). This is eaten with pita bread and is often accompanied by chicken or rabbit. You can ask for it in typical restaurants.

-**Kebab** (skewered grilled lamb). This is a very typical dish in Egypt and is normally accompanied by **Kofta** (ground lamb) in typical restaurants.

-**Shawarma**. This is the column of roast lamb or chicken from which slices are taken. It is often eaten in the form of a sandwich, with normal bread or pita, and mixed with salad.

-**Fatir** (Egyptian pancakes or pizza). Fatir is prepared with a large amount of dough with very fine flour that is filled with a salted ingredient like tuna or sausage, or a sweet ingredient, and then folded. Over this, cheese,

Making falafel. ■

onions and tomato are placed, after which it is baked in the oven.

Hors d'oeuvres and appetizers

Egyptian cuisine also offers a large variety of appetizers or "mezza", as the Egyptians call them, which are always served for nibbling before meals or accompanied by a drink. The most typical are:

-**Tahina**. Sesame sauce with vinegar, salt and pepper, which accompanies falafel, meat, chicken or fish.

187

■ Roast lamb, or kofta, mufafal rice and baklava.

-**Baba Ghanog**. A mix of roast eggplant and ground with sesame. On occasion, it has a little bit of parsley.
-**Zabadi.** Yoghurt sauce with a little bit of chopped mint or finely cut cucumber.
-**Vinaigrettes.** Egyptians accompany their food with spices, using turnips, carrots, olives, and chilli peppers.

■ Water melon seller.

Stall selling bananas. ■

Bread carrier.

–Grape leaves. These leaves are filled with rice, parsley and tomato, and lemon is squeezed on top.

Sweets

Although the usual dessert is fruit, Arab cuisine has many sweets like **Basbusa** (corn flour and coconut), **Konafa** (very fine noodles) and **Baklava** (layers of puff pastry), which are always elaborated with honey and nuts. Milk is often used, as in **rice with milk**, **Mahalabia** (cream) and **Um Ali** (puff pastry soaked in milk that is later baked in the oven).

Drinks

Tea is the most popular drink in Egypt. Normally, tea is served in homes without being asked. It is especially delicious when made with mint leaves.

Turkish coffee is also very common. The grains are ground with cardamom and the coffee is prepared with lots of grounds.

Karkade is another very common drink. It is prepared with hibiscus flower leaves and is drunk hot or cold.

Tamarind is drunk a lot in Cairo as a refreshing drink. In summer, it is normal to see all the street-side, tamarind vendors carrying a container on their back or on carts.

Natural juices, especially sugarcane, orange or mango, are served in many juice shops. Likewise, a delicious fruit cocktail **Fakhfakhina** is recommended.

Tamarind seller. ▪

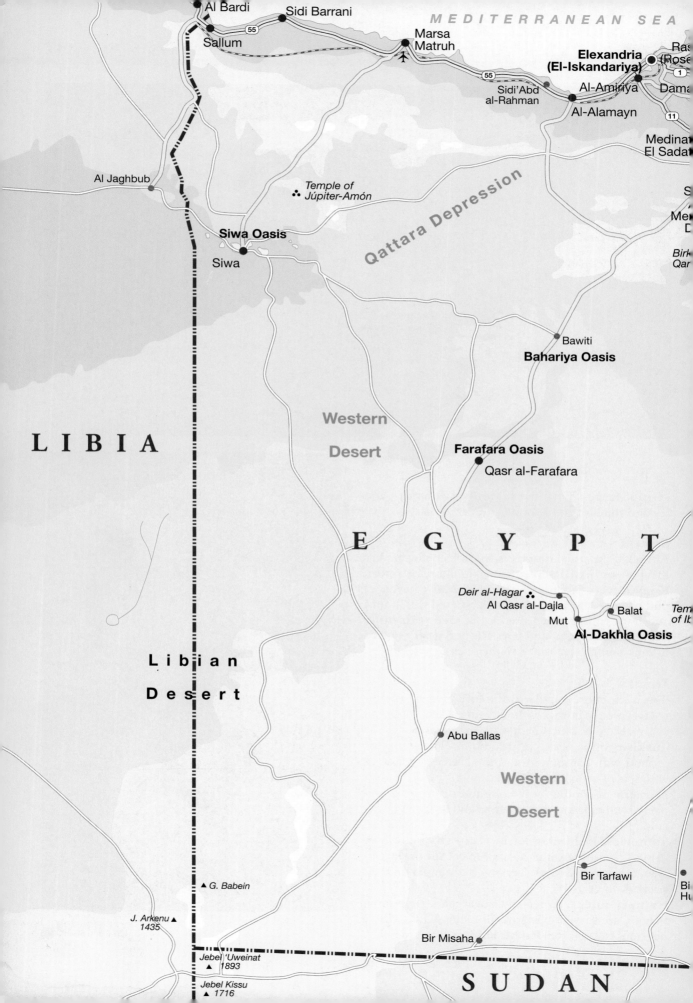